T0149066

BESPOKE

BESPOKE

A Guide to Cycle-Speak & Saddle Slang

TOM BROMLEY

BRITISH LIBRARY

Publisher's Note

Both Tom Bromley and British Library Publishing very much hope this will be the first of many editions of *BESPOKE*. We will certainly be keeping notes of new terms emerging from the rich and varied world of road cycling and invite you to make your own contributions for possible inclusion in future editions. Please email your suggestions to publishing_editorial@bl.uk or tweet us via @bl_publishing.

First published in Great Britain in 2021 by
The British Library
96 Euston Road
London NW1 2DB,
www.bl.uk

@bl_publishing

Edited by Anna Cheifetz
Design: Neil Stevens, Elaine Hewson and Georgina Hewitt
Illustrated by Neil Stevens
All photographs courtesy Offside/L'Équipe

A catalogue record for this book is available from the British Library

ISBN 978-0-7123-5365-6
Printed and bound in the Czech Republic by Finidr

Frontispiece: Fausto Coppi leads Jean Robic up
L'Alpe d'Huez in the 1952 Tour de France

Contents

ONE | A Few Words About Cycling

Some sports, it seems, are made for the written word. While it can feel that the likes of football, golf or tennis dominate the sports channels at times, they can never match the likes of boxing, say, or cycling when it comes to writing about the sports themselves. There is something about the combination of the romance, the history and the suffering that make these sports perfect for the page. A book like Norman Mailer's *The Fight* or Leonard Gardner's *Fat City* capture the essence of the sport, with their descriptions bringing boxing to life, and the fights spilling off the page and into the reader's imagination.

Cycling, too, has its fair share of great works – whether it is novels such as Tim Krabbé's *The Rider* or non-fiction works, such as Geoffrey Nicholson's *The Great Bike Race*. And while any cycling writer can draw on stories steeped in everything from bravery and heroism to double-crossing and downright skulduggery, in settings every bit as dramatic, what arguably makes this genre particularly special is the rich lexicon of cycling language an author can draw on.

Part of this comes from the continental origins of cycling, with strong cycling cultures developing initially in France, Italy and the Low Countries in particular. And while, as in so many sports, cycling has gone global in the past thirty or so years, the Anglicized presence of the Greg LeMonds or Bradley Wigginses has not diluted this culture as much as might have been expected. Instead, it has become customary for professional riders arriving from Africa and Australia, the USA and the UK to immerse themselves in cycling's prevailing language, culture and customs – those that do are welcomed and appreciated; those who don't can find themselves shunned in the peloton and with few friends on the side of the road.

For the cycling fan coming fresh to the sport, it can feel as if there is a bewildering number of terms to get their head around. Like many British fans of my generation, my induction into the sport came in the mid-1980s when Channel 4 started showing coverage of the Tour de France for the first time. It was a fortuitous era to discover cycling – who could not be compelled by the 1986 battle between Bernard Hinault and Greg LeMond, the 1987 confrontation between Stephen Roche and Pedro Delgado and the 1989 *tête-a-tête* between LeMond and Laurent Fignon?

My early guides were the commentators Phil Liggett and the late Paul Sherwen, who sadly died in 2018. Their commentaries introduced me to the specialised language of cycling, in which they were both fluent. As with so many other cycling fans, the Tour served as my gateway drug. Over the years cycling became more than just three weeks in July but stretched out to include the other Grand Tours (the Giro in May and the Vuelta in September), then the Classics from the first Monument of the spring (Milan–San Remo) to the Race of the Falling Leaves in the autumn, and beyond to include tours down under and in the desert at the start of the year, and finally, presentations of the following year's race routes in the off-season.

The aim of *BESPOKE* is to dig a little deeper into the words and phrases that form the vocabulary of cycling. It is intended to serve as an introduction to the sport for the new cycling fan and to provide the established fan with the stories behind the words they already know, hopefully introducing them to some new terms as well. Rather than listing terms alphabetically, I have placed them in themed chapters – from prizes to *parcours*, races to rider-types. The words, as with the sport itself, reflect a mixture of cultures – a French word here, an Italian term there. Some words are unique to one particular country, others have variations across different languages; some are so ubiquitous that they transcend borders to be internationally recognised terms.

Two small but important caveats. First, as always with a project of this kind, the length of the book precludes delving into every corner of cycling. As a result, the words featured in this book focus on road racing – and could easily have numbered more on that subject alone. The mysteries of track cycling and of the amateur world are too rich to just skim through here and must be saved for another day, and another volume. Because men's road racing has had more high-profile coverage during its history, many words – and therefore anecdotes – are derived from men's cycling. But with the increasing growth and pressure to raise the profile of women's cycling, inevitably new terms will follow and the language of cycling will no doubt evolve accordingly.

Secondly, as with any writer turning their attention to the story of cycling, there is the inevitable issue of cheating and drug-taking. It's something that has been part of the professional sport ever since its inception and as such I have dedicated a chapter to it here. On looking at the history of drugs in cycling over the years, the sport's inconsistent approach is noticeable. So while Lance Armstrong's seven Tour victories have been struck from his *palmarès*, other riders of the era who have admitted to doping (Bjarne Riis, for example) have not had their victories similarly expunged. Then there are cycling greats, such as Fausto Coppi and Jacques Anquetil, who have spoken publicly about their use of drugs during their racing careers. I'm certainly not here to defend Lance Armstrong, but with any telling of the story of cycling and drugs, it's too simplistic to make him and him alone *persona non grata*. Certainly, putting his career into context is not easy: it will be interesting to see how history treats the era of the 1990s and early 2000s in the years ahead.

A few words about the words about cycling. Given how cycling has developed as a sport, different terms in this book have different linguistic origins. Some terms have transcended their French/Italian/whatever roots to be the definitive term for a particular subject; in other cases, the different languages have adopted or retained their own variations. For each entry, I've tried to start with what seems to be the most commonly-used variant and to list the other translations underneath where relevant and distinct. So if the French/Italian/whatever equivalent is absent, it most likely means that a). it doesn't exist or b). its translation is so similar as to not be worth need repeating.

Cycling at its best offers the fan something few other sports can match – rivalry, romance, stories, scenery – it has, to borrow the word for winning in style, panache. *BESPOKE* is here to help you 'speak' cycling, to deepen your understanding of the language, the culture and history of this wonderful sport. Over the past few months it has been a pleasure to research and write this book; I hope you have as much enjoyment in reading it.

Tom Bromley

TWO | The Race

Imagine, if you will, the spread of a bike race during a stage of a Grand Tour. The ebb and flow as the riders stretch out creates a rhythm and language all of its own. There is a large difference between those at the front of the race, vying for the win, and those at the back, clinging on to stay in the race. Welcome to the world of buses, balls, black shirts and brooms...

TÊTE DE LA COURSE (FR)
Head of the Race (Eng)/*Testa Della Corsa* (It)/*Cabeza de Carrera* (Sp)

The person or people at the front of the race – the leader on the road. There's something fantastically descriptive about the language here, with the 'head' in top position and the 'body' as the peloton.

Over the course of a stage, the person or team at the head may vary from kilometre to kilometre. Early on, the riders at the front can oscillate wildly, as different riders attempt (and often fail) to get themselves in a breakaway that sticks. Then there are the savvier Thomas Voeckler types – the ones who get themselves in the later breakaway group, soaking up the applause of the fans and ensuring that their team's sponsor gets plenty of airtime: this has to be achieved after the first couple of hours when the TV coverage usually starts. Finally, there is the business end of the stage, where the general classification (GC) contenders or sprinters show their faces, depending on the type of terrain.

Back in the day, a cyclist with local roots who'd earned it would be allowed to ride ahead to greet friends and family. When the Tour de France passed through the UK in 1994, Sean Yates was allowed to cycle in advance of the race to greet his family: 'After asking Johan Museeuw for permission – he was in yellow [and] was the *de facto* boss of the race – I big-ringed it up the climb to where Mum, Dad, Uncle Michael, Chris, Ella, Conall and Oriana were all waiting for me with a bottle of champagne.'

There is also the romantic notion of the *tête de la course* meaning to ride from the front with style and panache. At the 1954 Tour de France, Federico Bahamontes (the Eagle of Toledo) reached the top of the Col de Romeyère in the Alps at the front of a four-man breakaway, fourteen minutes ahead of the peloton. He stopped, got off his bike and helped himself to an ice cream from a stall at the summit.

POURSUIVANT (FR)
Chaser(Eng)/*Inseguitore* (It)/*Achtevolger* (Nl)/*Perseguidor* (Sp)

'Just who is that rider coming up behind? Because that looks like Roche. That looks like Stephen Roche. It's Stephen Roche who's come over the line, he almost caught Pedro Delgado – I don't believe it!'

For British cycling fans of a certain vintage, Phil Liggett's commentary on the stage 21 of the 1987 Tour de France is forever etched in the collective memory (for some reason the Tour that year featured 25 stages plus a prologue, but let's not get distracted). The battle for victory was a straight fight between Pedro Delgado, winner of the 1985 Vuelta a Espana in somewhat controversial circumstances (see later) and Stephen Roche, hot from his victory in the 1986 Giro D'Italia (also in see later controversial circumstances).

When Roche didn't respond, Delgado quickly built up a two-minute lead – a Tour winning margin. But then came one of the great cycling chases. With five kilometres to go, Roche buried himself. Roche

was a *poursuivant* no-one saw coming, or indeed, no-one saw. Back then there were just two television bike cameras out on the road, one following the stage winner Laurent Fignon, the other tracking Pedro Delgado. Hence Phil Liggett's astonishment when Stephen Roche appeared around the final corner, just seconds behind Delgado. Roche collapsed over the line and was given oxygen in the back of an ambulance for 15 minutes, before emerging to declare *'Mais pas de femme ce soir'* ('No women for me tonight').

It's less glamorous, but winning stage races can be as much about the pursuers as the escapees, about minimising the losses and keeping the cycling powder dry for another day. That happened in 1987 – Roche went on to overturn Delgado's lead on the final time-trial – and it happened again in 2011, when Andy Schleck won the Tour's queen stage from Pinerolo to the summit of the Galibier with a wonderful, glorious 65-kilometre attack. Equally impressive in this race was the performance of Cadel Evans who, in full wasp-chewing mode, ground his way back into contention on the final slopes – cutting Schleck's four-and-a-half minute lead at the top of the penultimate mountain to just over two minutes at the finish. While record books show that Evans won the tour (Schleck lost it in the following time-trial in Grenoble), they don't note that it was this dogged pursuit in the shadow of Schleck's great ride that cemented his success.

BREAK/BREAKAWAY
Échappée, Échappée Fleuve, Échappée Bidon (Fr)/*Fuga, Fuga Bidone* (It)

Jacky Durand is a French cyclist with a modest *palmarès* (*see* Chapter Five) but with a reputation well beyond his achievements. A trio of Tour stage wins and a couple of French national championships aside, his biggest victory was a surprise win at the 1992 Tour of Flanders (*Ronde van Vlandereen*). Peter Cossins wonderfully describes Durand in *The Monuments* as 'a rider who regarded the waving of a start flag in the same way a cocker spaniel views their owner brandishing a stick. Almost as soon as it had dropped, "Dudu" would bound away, grinning like a loon, and riding like one too.'

If Durand has published a memoir, it should be called *It's All About The Break*. That for him was what cycling was about – escaping from the peloton and hoping to stay out ahead: 'I'd rather finish shattered and last having attacked a hundred times than finish 25th without having tried', he once told *L'Équipe*. Such was Durand's desire to cut loose that *Vélo* magazine famously ran a 'Jacky-metre', offering a monthly chart showing how long he spent in the breakaway. The Jacky-metre for the end of 2001 showed that he raced for 16,524 kilometres, out of which 2,270 kilometres had been spent in the break.

Very, very occasionally it worked. During the Tour of Flanders in 1992, Durand escaped as part of a group of four early on – and that means really early on. The group was whittled down to Durand and the Swiss rider Thomas Wegmuller with just the small matter of over 200 kilometres of the 256 kilometres route left to ride. It was suicidal cycling – no-one expected them to last and so the duo were left to stretch their lead to 23 minutes. By the time the peloton reacted it was too late: Durand attacked Wegmuller, with the rest finishing three minutes behind.

Breakaways come in all shapes and sizes. Whether they work depends on who is in them. The lengthy solo break is the stuff of legend. On the 19th stage of the 2018 Giro D'Italia, Chris Froome attacked early on the slopes of the Colle Delle Finestre and stayed out in front for the next 80 km, helped by some carefully placed Team Sky helpers, waiting ahead with sufficient fuel to keep him going. He jumped from fourth to first in the overall standings and went on to win the race. At the 1946 Milan–San Remo, Fausto Coppi joined the early breakaway just outside Milan and emerged from the Turchino tunnel alone, riding the remaining 90 miles solo and beating the second-placed rider by 14 minutes.

If Coppi hadn't been there, this early group of escapees could have been an example of what the Italians call a *Fuga Bidone* and the French an *Échappée Bidon* – an early break of unfancied riders whose chances of success are somewhere between limited and non-existent (the *bidon* here comes from the French for 'phoney', rather than the more common cycling term for water bottle).

The group breakaway with the best chance of success is the *Échappée Fleuve*, which poetically translates as 'river escape'. Rather than a weekend away by the banks of the Loire, the *Échappée Fleuve* is a movement where the breakaway group works together so that a flow of riders take their turn at the front as they try to hold off the peloton. Who is in the breakaway determines who is going to put in a shift at the front of the peloton to bring them back. During the 2012 Olympic Road Race, a group of about 20 riders managed to get away by the final lap, representing most of the major countries in the race. The British team found that few helpers volunteered to bring the race back together, because everyone knew that would probably allow Mark Cavendish to sprint to victory.

It is unusual for a breakaway that large to keep away from the peloton. In *The World of Cycling According to G*, Geraint Thomas notes, 'Get more than ten riders in an escape and it will be less likely to work. More people will slip turns. There'll be less cohesion. Get six to eight in there and it will be the toughest to chase down, because every one of that group will commit.' (The Olympic road race was a slightly special case as each team only had five riders, making control of the race more difficult).

There are lots of other variables that determine whether a breakaway is successful. Some days are more breakaway friendly than others – breakaways are less likely to work on the flat, as the sprinter teams have a vested interested in keeping the race together; likewise in the mountains, when the general classification (GC) riders come to the fore. It is when the road map is more mixed, a bit bobbly to balance out the power of the peloton or the punch of the climbers, that a break is more likely to maintain its lead.

Even with the requisite number of riders, the chance of a successful break depends on who is in it. Any big names make it far less likely to succeed (unless they've had such a terrible race that they're no longer in contention). Get more than one member of the same team in a breakaway and the tactics can change – one or other saving their legs for the finish. Sometimes there are also larger strategies at play: a GC rider might send a teammate up the road as part of a planned attack later on in the stage – so that when they try to bridge the gap, there will be help waiting for them in the breakaway.

CHASSE PATATE (FR)

Between the break and the peloton are the riders stuck between the two – those who have broken free of the peloton but aren't doing enough to make it up to the breakaway. The term literally means 'chasing potatoes' and there are different accounts of its origins. Some suggest it derives from cyclists stuffing themselves

with food and being too weighed down to catch up with the race again afterwards. More prosaically, the term may have its origins in the fact that *patate* is also slang for idiot or blockhead.

PELOTON (FR)
Il Gruppo (It)/The Bunch (Eng)

'You join me in the helicopter as we look down on these cyclists that look like cattle in some mad way, but cattle on bikes.' Alan Partridge commentating during his time as a sports reporter for *The Day Today*, with his own inimitable take on a mass of cyclists; known by everyone else, of course, as the peloton.

Peloton is a French word, but one that has crossed into most languages – a cycling term that even Clarkson-loving non-cycling fans know. It comes from *pelote*, a sixteenth-century word meaning a pellet or small ball of wool or thread. Over the centuries its meaning evolved to signify a small group of soldiers – leading to the term platoon. As cycling began to develop and grow as a sport, it became the term for a group of riders. The 1909 Tour de France, which included teams as well as individual cyclists for the first time, is usually taken as the point when the term came into common coinage.

The peloton today is the main body of riders on the road. But it is also used to refer to the riders in a race en masse. In cases where the race breaks down, you can also have a succession of smaller pelotons. Pellets? Or maybe that's just balls. Either way, it's a fluid term, a little like the mass of riders, changing shape and formation as the route, the weather and the race furniture demand.

Michael Barry, the former US Postal rider, once wrote that, 'the peloton flows with the roads... A wall of wheels and bodies means we can never see too far in front, so we trust that the peloton flows around any obstacle in the road like fish in a current.' In his book *The Rider*, David Millar also describes the peloton as once being 'an organic, flowing thing', but more recently something more 'robotic' thanks to the demands of team *directeurs* – and more often than not only a slip of a pedal away from being 'a total clusterfuck.'

Millar recalls that back in the day, riders would find their natural place in the peloton and the group would move along naturally as one – no longer individual riders or even a team, but one organic mass. Once team orders are barked out, everyone starts getting in everyone else's way. It only takes a touch of wheels for a whole load of riders to go down like a pack of dominoes. To minimize that risk, everyone wants their protected riders up towards the front of the peloton, out of potential trouble. But of course not everyone can be up near the front, hence the scrabble for places, the heightened nervousness, and the higher likelihood of crashes. It's a sort of self-fulfilling prophecy.

When the peloton is in full flight, it is one of the most beautiful sights in cycling, or indeed in sport full stop. Such is the effect of slipstreaming that those nestled within the group can find themselves expending substantially less energy (up to 40 per cent less) than those pulling their turn on the front. Such is the peloton's power that it can often pull in a breakaway rider at will. Much of road racing is about letting a rider sit out front at a distance that is catchable, but far enough ahead to deter others from joining in. Like a cat toying with a mouse, when the peloton want to reel a rider in, they usually can. Rare indeed is the rider who can escape from the peloton at full steam. Tony Martin gave it a go at the 2013 Vuelta, leading to a memorable battle between a world time-trial champion and the peloton at full speed. It was touch and go, but they caught him with 100 metres to go.

ECHELONS (FR)
Éventail (Fr) / *Bordure* (Fr) / *Ventaglio* (It)
Stage 13 of the 2013 Tour de France was meant to be a day off for the GC contenders, a comparatively gentle roll across the undulating countryside from Tours to Saint-Amand-Montrond. But no-one had accounted for the havoc wreaked on the peloton by crosswinds. When the wind blows from left to right or right to left, the power of the peloton's arrowhead formation is ineffective. In these conditions, the way to save energy is to ride in a rolling, overlapping diagonal line from one side of the road to the other – an echelon. The front rider takes on the bulk of the wind before pulling off to let the next rider do their stint. Echelons equal gaps, sometimes big gaps – once an echelon is away, it's nigh on impossible to pull it back. On a day of crosswinds, if you're not at the front and paying attention, all the hard work put in over the course of a tour can be, well, blown away.

Back to the 2013 Tour. Alejandro Valverde, lying second behind race leader Chris Froome, got a puncture. The Belkin team, who had two riders in the top

five, put the hammer down. With Marcel Kittel off the back of the peloton as well, the other sprint teams joined in the drive. Then a sharp-eyed Saxo Bank team noticed that Froome was sitting a way down the peloton. Contador and his teammates accelerated and a gap of 30 metres appeared. Froome sprinted to try to catch them and failed to get across. By the time Contador's group reached the finish line, Froome had lost over a minute to one of his main rivals. Valverde, meanwhile, lost ten minutes and was out of contention.

During the Vuelta, a visit to Albacete and the flatlands of La Mancha pretty much guarantees what the Spanish call *abacinos*. In the third stage of the 1996 race the crosswinds caused the peloton to split into two; two of the pre-race favourites, Tony Rominger and Fernando Escartín, found themselves at the back of the group and echeloned to the tune of seven minutes. 'All year spent working to win the Vuelta and then along comes one of these stages – in principle short and unimportant – and I lose everything', a tearful Escartín said afterwards.

On the stage to Guadalajara at the 2019 Vuelta, it was the turn of race leader Primoz Roglic to get caught out. On a day of strong crosswinds, the peloton split after just 3 km of the 220 km stage. Forty riders went clear, including almost the entire Deceunicek-Quick Step team and Nairo Quintana, who on a climb-free day gained more time on his GC rivals than he had in all the mountain stages put together. Roglic, stuck behind in the second group on the road, lost over five minutes.

GRUPPETTO (IT)
Autobus (Fr)/Laughing Group (Eng/US)

Most commonly known as the *gruppetto*, but also the *autobus* or laughing group, this is the group of riders behind the main peloton who have little interest in contesting that day's stage, but every interest in doing just enough to stay in the race for another day. It might be a Cav-type sprinter who can't climb, wanting to

make it through the mountains for the final sprint down the Champs-Élysées. It could be a *domestique* who has done their bit for the day for the team leader. Or perhaps a rider who is just having an off-day and hasn't got the stomach for the business end of a stage.

The key person in the *gruppetto* is the cyclist who is good at maths. Because staying in the race means riding home within the agreed time limit. That's not a straightforward calculation. The Tour de France rulebook divides its stages into six different types from 'stages with no particular difficulty' to 'very difficult short stages', with a coefficient for each that can be used to calculate a time limit, depending on the average speed. So if the stage is 'a short stage with uneven terrain', then you need to refer to Coefficient 3; and if the average speed of the race is 39-40 kilometres per hour, then the time limit for the day will be the winner's finish time plus 15 per cent. Should the winner roll in on exactly four hours, then the time limit for the day will be four hours and 36 minutes if you want to be on the start line for the following day.

If you're in the *gruppetto* for working that out, you wouldn't be alone. Thankfully, when the maths gets tough or the hills get tougher, the *gruppetto* has a get-out clause in terms of numbers: if enough riders finish outside the time limit – over 20 per cent – then the race organizers can, and usually do, let them back in. So

— the illustration of a cyclist appears in the left margin of the page.

as long as you do a head count of 30-40 riders, then you're usually okay. Such was the case during Andy Schleck's epic ride up the Galibier in the 2011 Tour (see *Breakaway* above) – a total of 89 riders failed to make the time limit, but were allowed back in.

MAGLIA NERA (IT)

During the Giro d'Italias of the late 1940s, the headline battle was between two cycling greats – Gino Bartali and Fausto Coppi. But at the back of the race, another competition also caught the public's imagination – the battle for the *Maglia Nera* or black shirt. The black shirt, of course, had a historical connotation or two in the aftermath of the Second World War and Mussolini's fascist rule. So making the last placed rider in the race wear a black shirt was deliberately symbolic – rather than the black shirt demanding respect, it was now the hallmark of the loser.

Except that, in one of those strange quirks of cycling, the *tifosi* (fans, *see* Chapter Eight) became rather fond of the wearer of the jersey – in an ironic, rather than a political way. Luigi Malabrocca was the first to work out that he could get a certain level of fame and notoriety from finishing bottom of the GC, rather than anonymously in the middle of it. As with the *gruppetto*, the *maglia nera* wearer had to ensure that they stayed within the time limit, but unlike the *gruppetto* rider, who might finish one day at the back and another day sprint for the line, the last placed rider did their best to ensure that they finished last *every* day and thus held on to the jersey. Long after the leaders had crossed the finish line, the *tifosi* would wait (and wait) at the finish line for Malabrocca to arrive – as would the bored timekeepers, who threatened to go on strike if the award wasn't dropped, which it was in 1951.

By 1949, Malabrocca had a rival for his 'crown' in the form of Luigi Carollo. Thus began a somewhat comic slow bicycle race within a race. Malabrocca had a policeman cousin who helped him calculate the time limit and wend his way through the reopened roads; Carollo wore two watches to keep track of the time. Such was the rivalry that the pair would hide from each other in order to slip into last place. In *Pedlare! Pedlare!* John Foot recounts one bizarre episode when Malabrocca hid from Carollo in a water tank, 'only to be discovered by a local peasant, an episode which inspired this surreal dialogue: 'What are you doing?' 'Riding the Giro.' 'In my tank?''

Malabrocca's hopes of winning his third *maglia nera* were scuppered on the final day, having finally stretched the timekeeper's patience too far. After stopping to chat to locals in one rural town bar (and finding the time to admire one of the regulars' fishing equipment), Malabrocca rolled up two hours behind the stage winner, only to discover the timekeepers were no longer there. Bored of waiting with their stopwatches, they gave him the same time as the main bunch and had gone home. The result was that the jersey went to Carollo, a mere ten hours behind Fausto Coppi.

The last winner of the *maglia nera* was Giovanni Pinarello in 1951. Yes, that Pinarello: retiring the following year, he set about making his own bikes, opening his first shop in 1953. These days, Pinarello is all about riding the *tête de la course* rather than off the back of the peloton: Miguel Indurain won all of his Tour de France titles riding a Pinarello, as did Sir Bradley Wiggins in 2012.
(See also *Lanterne Rouge*, Chapter Five)

VOITURE BALAI (FR)
Broom Wagon (Eng)/*Carro Scopa* (It)/*Coche Escobar* (Sp)
In 1910, the Tour de France tackled a whole string of Pyrenean peaks for the first time. The Cols de Peyresourde, Aspin, Aubisque and Tourmalet might be (cycling) household names today, but they were relatively unknown to the peloton. A number of riders were unhappy at the proposed route – Octave Lapize famously shouted 'Assasins!' at officials on the Tourmalet for putting him through the ordeal.

To reassure riders about their safety, and that they wouldn't be left to find their own way home should they decide to abandon, the race organizers introduced the *voiture balai* (the 'broom wagon') to ride at the back of the race and 'sweep up' any riders who wanted to give up. The van had a broom strapped to its roof – something that continued until the early 1990s – and quickly became part of cycling tradition.

Getting off the bike and into the wagon is about as humiliating as it gets for a rider. On that famous day in 1987, when Stephen Roche was experiencing one of his best days on the bike on the slopes of La Plagne (see *Poursuivants*), his fellow Irishman Paul Kimmage was having one of his worst. Riding for the RMO team, he struggled up the Lauteret before finding himself overtaken on the Galibier by 'a bearded tourist, riding up the mountain with pannier bags on his bike.' Unable to keep up with the race, he describes the broom wagon sitting right behind him 'like a magnet.' Looking for a space when he could climb into the wagon without anyone watching, he eventually abandonned the race at the foot of the Col du Télégraphe.

Before a cyclist can get into the wagon, there is the ritual of removing the rider's race numbers. Persona non grata, Kimmage found himself driven along

Above Jean Robic, closely
pursued by the Broom Wagon
at the 1959 Tour de France

the remaining route through the fans to the finish line. In *Rough Ride,* he says, 'I pull the blanket around myself again, this time to hide my identity. I am in disgrace.' At the finish, he hears his name read out among the list of abandonments by the race announcer: 'his voice is soft and sad. The tones are those you would expect from a man announcing a list of soldiers killed in a war.'

Of course, not everyone ends up in the broom wagon: team leaders tend to opt for the team car instead, as Chris Froome did when he abandoned in 2014. But for the regular riders, the broom wagon is an experience that most go through at least once in their career – and never want to again.

THREE | The Riders

Tim Krabbé's novel *The Rider* is probably the best novel ever written about cycling. If you haven't read it, you should. This chapter is not trying to be a sequel to that book, but is a look at the different types of rider found in road-racing, from road captains to *rouleurs*, *puncheurs* to *poisson pilotes*. Cycling might be a team sport, but each team is made up of a remarkable number of individual types.

PATRON (FR)

The Tour de France 2012, Stage 14 from Limoux to Foix. Cadel Evans, the Australian rider who always seemed to be grimacing even when he was winning, was not in the best of moods. His defence of his Tour title was crumbling in the face of Sky double act Bradley Wiggins and Chris Froome, while BMC teammate Tejay Van Garderen was making 'next generation' noises and asking to be given his head. Then to rub salt into his wounds, or more accurately, sharp metal into rubber, Evans punctured. Someone – obviously not the world's biggest cycling fan – had sprayed the summit of the Mur de Péguère with tacks. Evans waited patiently for a teammate to give him his bike, only for that to have been attacked too. If his Tour defence was already sinking, it was now well and truly sunk.

Enter Bradley Wiggins. Wiggo is a man who knows his cycling history and as leader of the race, stepped up to take control of the proceedings. The leaders would wait for Evans to sort himself out he decided: 'it was the honourable thing to do', he said. So when a young Pierre Roland broke away from the peloton – acting unhonourably – Wiggo and Sky went hell for leather to reel him back in.

In the grand scheme of the race, the episode didn't affect the final outcome: Evans ended up finishing seventh, fifteen minutes down (though one place ahead of Pierre Roland, which seemed a sort of cycling karma). But on this stage Wiggins had demonstrated his desire to take on the role of patron.

A patron is the cyclist who leads the peloton. That's different to being top of the GC. A rider can be a patron without winning the race; equally, a rider can dominate a race without being the patron. The patron is someone who has the authority to dictate how the rest of the peloton behaves; who will reinforce the old-fashioned etiquette of cycling yore (not attacking your opponent when he is disadvantaged through no fault of his own); who decides whether the peloton will take it fast or easy, and have it in their patronage to let a breakaway escape or not; and who will represent the riders when the peloton is feeling hard done by. It's a position that is part mafia boss, part Grand Tour winner, part shop steward and part showman.

The patron's patron is Bernard Hinault. In his first Tour de France in 1978, the peloton took umbrage at a ridiculous (and money-making) schedule: a split-stage day that saw a 7.30am start for a 160 kilometre stage to Valance, then a second afternoon stage of 96 kilometres to Toulouse; all hemmed in between lengthy transfers the night before and the morning after. The response of the peloton was to down tools and walk in Valance, to the fury of the local mayor who had forked out thousands to stage a race finish. Hinault led the riders in, squared up to the mayor and took the boos and tomatoes of the crowd in his stride. On the 1984 Tour, the stage to La Seyne-sur-Mer was blocked by striking dockers. Once again Hinault took control, charging into them full steam, punching and kicking anyone who got in his way.

Of course a patron can use his power for better or for worse. While Wiggo's attempts to neutralize the race in 2012 to help Cadel Evans showed good patronage, Lance Armstrong's treatment of Filippo Simeoni in the 2004 Tour was less noble. Armstrong had a beef with Simeoni over comments he'd made about Armstrong's doctor, Michele Ferrari, so when Simeoni attempted to join the breakaway, Armstrong went with him. With the *maillot jaune* (*see* Chapter Five) in the leading group, the breakaway stood no chance of succeeding. Armstrong said he would only drop back if Simeoni went with him, which the Italian reluctantly did. Simeoni said afterwards that, 'a big champion like him can't possibly do something like that to a small rider like me' – a response that was both right and wrong at the same time. Armstrong could behave like that because as patron he had the power to do so; but as patron he shouldn't have used that power for personal point-scoring. (For other things Armstrong shouldn't have done, *see* Chapter Thirteen.)

CAMPIONISSIMO (IT)

There are champions. And then there are super-champions, the champions of champions. The *campionissimo*. The term was originally coined to describe the efforts of the early twentieth-century Italian cyclist Constante Girardengo. Giradengo was a hugely popular and successful cyclist in the years following the First World War. He was sometimes called 'Mr San Remo' on account of winning the Milan–San Remo six times in ten years. He was sometimes called 'Gira' for his Giro winning exploits (do you see what they did there?), including leading the race from start to finish in 1919.

Following on from Girardengo, the next *campionissimo* was Alfredo Binda – a cyclist who so dominatated the Giro d'Italia in the late 1920s (winning 26 out 41 stages from 1927 to 1929) that in 1930 the organizers decided the race would be a forgone conclusion if he turned up and so paid him the winner's fee not to compete in the race. Another world war later and the *campionissimo* tag was dusted down for another Italian great – *the* Italian great, Fausto Coppi. Coppi won five Giros, two Tour de Frances (including the double twice), eight Monuments (three Milan–San Remos, five Tour of Lombardys) and the world title in 1953. No Italian cyclist has matched the achievements of Coppi – until they do, he is *il campionissimo* for the forseeable future.

PROTECTED RIDER

Cycling might be a team sport, but it's a team sport geared around its leaders, with supporters – *domestiques* or *gregari* (*see* below) – to do their bidding. Every budding rider dreams of being afforded protected rider status, which will relieve them of schlepping back to the team car for another bidon for His Cycleness and allow them to concentrate on the business of racing.

Quite who the protected rider is will depend on the objectives of the team. It could be a GC contender. It could be a sprinter. It could be someone with designs on a specific jersey or a Classics rider with a shout at outright victory. It could be someone who has earned it after the hard graft of *domestique* servitude. After burying himself for Chris Froome in 2015, and with the departure of Richie Porte to follow his own GC ambitions, Geraint Thomas found himself upgraded to a protected GC rider for the 2016 season. Two years later, Thomas and Froome were

the team's co-leaders at the Tour, with Thomas proving triumphant: the following year, Thomas saw his title fall to another protected rider, Egan Bernal.

How many protected riders a team can have at any one race is a debatable question. When Team Sky signed Mark Cavendish for the 2012 season, the pre-race talk focused on how the team were going to win both the green and yellow jerseys for Cavendish and Wiggins respectively. But those twin aims required different personnel. Sean Yates in his memoir says, 'As a *directeur sportif* trying to win the [2012] Tour de France, having Cav on the team was frankly an inconvenience.' That was made clear on stage 6 when he didn't wait for Cavendish, who was stuck behind a crash, preferring to drive ahead to make sure he was there if Wiggins needed him. For Cavendish, who already felt hard done by over the number of *domestiques* assigned to him, it was pretty much the final straw in their relationship.

The situation was part of an anything-is-possible, aim high approach by Team Sky, but in this case the home truths of traditional cycling held firmer – have one protected rider and shape the team around them. Anyone else in the team who is protected should be a plan B option, someone who is able to slip into the same role rather than being skilled at something different.

Perhaps when having more than one protected rider, it is easier when those riders are cut from the same cloth: Team Sky/Ineos achieved that in 2018/19, with their co-leaders duking it out until it became clear which of the riders had the strongest legs. Quite how many protected riders cut from the same cloth a team can effectively support is another question: Movistar went one better than Team Sky/Ineos Ineos for the 2018/9 Tours by selecting a trident of potential GC winners in their teams: their best-placed riders, however, could only finish sixth and seventh respectively.

POISSON PILOTE (FR)
Lead Out Man (Eng)

What Cavendish lacked in the 2012 Sky team was his traditional lead out man or *poisson pilote* (the 'pilot fish'). This is the final part of The Train (*see* Chapter Twelve), that seamless team set up that takes a sprinter to the front of the bunch with 200 metres to go. The *poisson pilote* is the last link in this chain – and most successful sprinters have this unsung second-in-command hero to thank for their victories.

For Cavendish, it is the Australian Mark Renshaw; for Djamolidine Abdujaparov it was Guido Bontempi; for Mario Cipollini it was Giovanni Lombardi. Quite often the *passion pilote* has some sprinting temperament themselves. Sometimes it is an older hand helping out a younger colleague (as Alessandro Petacchi did for Cavendish at Omega Pharma Quick-Step); sometimes it is a role taken by an up-and-coming sprinter (as Matt Goss did for Cavendish at HTC-Columbia when Renshaw was unavailable). Having a lead out man who can sprint can be a useful fallback when things go wrong: so when Cavendish felt off colour at the 2014 Tour of Britain, Renshaw could step in and sprint for the stage victory.

A *poisson pilote* doesn't just bury themselves for their sprinter, they can also use their position at the front of the race to impede the chances of others. At the 2010 Tour, Renshaw went head-to-head and elbow-to-elbow with rival lead out man Julian Dean to get Cavendish into position, before dropping back into the path of Dean's sprinter, Tyler Farrar, impeding him in the process. Cavendish won the stage, but Renshaw found himself disqualified for his efforts in helping his man.

DOMESTIQUE (FR)
Gregario (It)

Back in the early years of the Tour de France, the race was seen as an individual event. It was an ongoing battle for creator Henri Desgrange to dissuade alliances or teams forming, and one that he would eventually lose. But not before various riders were disqualified for helping others and one of cycling's most famous terms was created.

At the 1911 Tour de France, French rider Maurice Brocco found his race effectively over after one particularly disastrous stage. Out of the running, he decided to offer his services to other riders. François Faber was facing elimination and so Brocco acted as his pacemaker, keeping Faber within the time limit. This outraged Desgrange to the point that he famously declared: '*C'est une domestique.*' ('he is no more than a servant'). Piqued, Brocco told Desgrange at the start of the stage to Bayonne that 'today, we are going to settle our accounts' and won the *étape* by 34 minutes. Desgrange promptly disqualified him on the grounds that that he had been helping others earlier in the race.

Brocco's Tour might have been over, but Desgrange's insult to him lived on. When Desgrange lost his battle to keep the Tour from being a team event, it was the term *domestique* that was adopted to describe those at the behest of their team leader. In football, the term 'water carrier' has been used to describe a certain type of player since 1996 when Eric Cantona used it for Didier Deschamps – meaning a team player there to pass the ball to the better players. But in cycling, the *domestique* has been fetching water for his team leader for the best part of a century.

In Italy, the equivalent term *gregario* means 'supporter' or 'follower' and Italian cycling seems to have accepted the importance of these selfless grafters earlier than the French. According to John Foot's *Pedlare! Pedlare!*, Constante

Girandengo had a team of dedicated *gregari* helping him to win while Desgrange was still trying to outlaw such behavior in France. By the 1940s Gina Bartali (Giovanni Corrieri) and Fausto Coppi (Andrea Carrea, Ettore Milano) had their loyal lieutenants by their side at all times. Their devotion was such that when Carrea found himself in yellow at the 1952 Tour de France (following team orders to sit in the break), he was distraught at upstaging his leader. The following day he was photographed polishing Coppi's shoes whilst wearing the yellow jersey to make his position clear. Coppi won that day's first ever climb of Alpe d'Huez so, to Carrea's relief, order was restored.

For every *domestique* tale of subordination and cycling suffrage, there are plenty more of cyclists frustrated with team orders and wanting to race for themselves. Bradley Wiggins and Chris Froome at the 2012 Tour is just one case in a long line of such examples, with team leaders gnashing their teeth at their teammate's behaviour. Similarly, there was the case of Roberto Visentini and Stephen Roche at the 1987 Giro; while in the 1986 Tour, Bernard Hinault's promise to help Greg LeMond as a sort of *super-domestique* in return for his support the previous year was hard to discern as he attacked the race off the front.

Back in 1962, Jacques Anquetil attempted to add the Vuelta title to his Tour and Giro triumphs. His team of *domestiques* included a young Rudi Altig, smarting from being told by team bosses that he was too inexperienced to be considered for that year's Tour de France. But when Altig found himself in the leader's jersey, his attitude was somewhat different to Andrea Carrea. Altig refused to budge, even using some secret planning to beat Anquetil at the time-trial, his specialist event. Anquetil retired, citing a gastric infection, though it was the disloyalty of his teammate that probably turned his stomach.

The *domestique* might not get the glory – indeed some *domestiques*' duties are over before the television cameras even start rolling. But their hard work is not in vain as any prize money and bonuses are usually split between the team as a reward for their efforts. Note the 'usually': such was the rift between Wiggins and Froome that after the 2012 Tour, Wiggins gave all his teammates their share of the prize money and bonuses – except for Froome. (Froome eventually received his share from Wiggins a year later.)

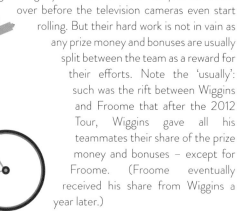

CAPITAINE DE ROUTE (FR)
Road Captain (Eng)

The role of a captain in cycling is different to that of other sports. The road captain isn't the leader in terms of cycling ability, but the one pulling the strings to ensure that the team's plans are carried out. They're usually an experienced rider getting towards the end of their career; one whose knowledge of the sport can be used to read the race and adapt the team's tactics accordingly.

David Millar, who become a road captain late in his career (including for the GB team at the 2011 World Championships and the 2012 Olympic road race), says of his role in the *The Rider*: 'I may have lost my ability to continuously deliver results, but at the same time I have such a depth of knowledge that I can read races better than anyone else in the team and have never been afraid to make decisions and call the shots on the road. Most importantly, I am still strong enough to be at the front of the race in key moments when the most important decisions have to be made.'

A curious mix of attributes is required: you've got to be a tough character, not only to cajole your teammates but also to stay up with the action – you're not much use as a road captain if you're hanging off the back of the peloton, struggling to keep up. Your eyes have to be open to who is having a bad day, while ensuring that you don't have one yourself. There's a question in the modern era of whether the *Capitaine de Route* has lost some of his influence now that everyone is radioed up. Arguably the *directeur sportif* (*see* Chapter Eight) calls the shots from the comfort of his car with the road captain just reinforcing the decisions in the peloton. But that ignores the skill of the road captain in reading the race – unlike the *directeur sportif*, he is the one in the thick of it, using his eyes and know-how to assess how the race is unfolding. Sometimes that little bit of knowledge – and a spur of the moment decision – can be the difference between winning and losing.

BAROUDEUR (FR)
Attacante (It)

'There is no set format for a *baroudeur*,' Paul Fournel helpfully offers in *Vélo*, his wonderful collection of cycling essays. 'Neither a true sprinter, nor a true climber, nor exactly a *rouleur*, the *baroudeur* is all of those at once,' he continues to blur the picture still further. 'He is capable of all of it, but in his own time. He knows that he will not beat the sprinters at the finish and so he has to set off beforehand. He knows that he will not beat the climbers in the high mountains; he makes his kingdom in the medium mountains.'

A *baroudeur* is less of a cyclist with a particular talent and more one with a specific sense of spirit and adventure. They are riders who are 'talented, courageous and clever' as William Fotheringham once put it. They're not going to outsprint a sprinter or out-climb a climber, but they can outfox them both by taking a risk, getting in a breakaway, giving their all and seeing what happens.

We're talking about riders like Jacky Durand, Tony Gallopin, Thomas Voeckler, Sandy Casar or Jens Voigt. At the 2010 Tour de France, stage 9 was a classic *baroudeur* win: both Voigt and Casar were up in a breakaway group of ten after just 30 kilometres. As the stage headed over various peaks towards the Madeleine the group was whittled down, but even as the main favourites caught up, Casar had just enough left to sprint ahead for the victory – a talented, courageous and clever win all wrapped up in one.

If the *baroudeur* had a natural habitat, it would be in the lesser hills. Here, they are more likely to get away and stay away; a landscape where the stage is neither flat or steep enough for the sprinter and GC teams to take charge and reel them back in.

ROULEUR (FR)
Passista (It)

Literally, a roller. As described by *Velominati.com*, a *rouleur* 'is a rider who goes well on flat and rolling terrain. They are characterized less by their size than by their style on the machine. A magnificent stroke tuned to sustained power, not high revolutions or bursts of acceleration'. It's this capacity to grind out kilometre after kilometre of power that often makes *rouleurs* good time-triallists, good all-rounders and a good bet when the course suits them, such as Paris–Roubaix. It's no coincidence that Fabian Cancellara has won the 'Hell of the North' on multiple occasions.

If Cancellara is a modern-day *rouleur*, then five times Tour winner Jacques Anquetil is the classic example. When he won the 1962 Tour after a dominant display in the final time-trial, Henri Derrigade described him as 'definitely the best *rouleur* in the world.' Three years later *L'Équipe* went one better, calling Anquetil 'worthy of being considered the greatest *rouleur* of all time,' after he won that year's *Dauphiné* then immediately got on a plane from Avignon to Bordeaux in time for the start of Bordeaux–Paris in the middle of the night. Anquetil won the longest one-off race at 557 kilometres in just over fifteen hours.

GRIMPEUR (FR)
Climber (Eng)/*Scalatore* (It)/*Escalador* (Sp)/*Escarabajos* (Col)

These are the climbers, the ones who are good at going uphill. The pure climbers tend to be small, light-as-a-feather things – handy for climbs as they've got less bodyweight to heave over the top, but less good on the flat where their lack of kilograms means they can't compete with the engine and big gears of a *rouleur*.

In Colombian cycling riders such as Nairo Quintana or Luis Herrera are known as *escarabajos* or beetles. The Spanish rider Federico Bahamontes is a classic *grimpeur*. He was the first rider to win the King of the Mountains title in all three Grand Tours and won it in the Tour de France six times between 1954 and 1964. Yet his inability to descend (see below) or to time-trial meant that for all his remarkable uphill gains, he only ever managed to convert this remarkable mountain dominance into one major title – the 1959 Tour de France. A similar fate befell a generation of Colombian climbers in the 1980s. Like Bahamontes, Luis Herrera won the King of the Mountains title in all three Grand Tours but only achieved one overall Grand Tour victory in the 1987 Vuelta.

DÉGRINGOLEUR (FR)
Dicesista (It)
What goes up must come down. Unless it's a mountain-top finish, of course. How you descend from a climb can be as important as tackling its slope in the first place. There's plenty of time to be won or lost, depending how good you are. If you are a *dégringoleur* – an expert descender – then the rewards can be high. If you're not, then losing time might be the least of your worries.

Gaston Nencini (the 'Lion of Mughello'), who won the Giro in 1957 and the Tour in 1960, was one of the great descenders. 'The only reason to follow Nencini downhill,' Raphael Geminiani once said, 'would be if you had a death wish.' That sounds like hyperbole, but the 1960 Tour favourite Roger Rivière made the mistake of trying to follow him down the Col de Perjuret in the Pyrenees. He misjudged a corner, fell forty feet into a ravine and was paralysed for life. When Luis Ocaña attempted to follow another *dégringoleur,* Eddy Merckx, on another rain-soaked Pyrenean descent he was also outdone, crashing out of the race lead and indeed the race.

Cycling is littered with examples of great climbers who were also terrible descenders – Federico Bahamontes and Andy Schleck are just two examples. Bahamontes even built in the fact that he was going to lose time, using the descent as a time to refuel and take food on board, so he was ready to attack once the roads went uphill again. Sometimes riders simply lose their nerve, as Bradley Wiggins did, to his great cost, at the 2013 Giro after a crash on the greasy mountain roads.

But done right, descending can be a wonderful thing. As Geraint Thomas said in his memoir, 'never do you feel more at one with your bike that when you are

Above Federico Bahamontes leads
Charly Gaul over the top of the
Tourmalet, 1959 Tour de France

descending... as a pro chasing wins I still get the same excitement and thrill from
hammering down hills as I did as a kid.'

PUNCHEUR (FR)

A *puncheur* is a cyclist with, well, punch. Not in a pugilistic sense but in his legs,
with the power to welly up a climb at high speed. It's impact cycling. *Puncheurs*
aren't built for the long climbs of the Alps and Pyrenees but a short sharp incline,
like the 20 per cent slope of the Mur de Huy, as featured in La Flèche Wallonne
and on stage 3 of the 2015 Tour de France, is their classic territory.

Indeed, if the *puncheur* had a favourite week of the year it is probably Ardennes
Week – that part of the Classics calendar that takes cycling through three races
in seven days in Belgium and the Netherlands: Amstel Gold, La Flèche Wallonne
and Liège–Bastogne–Liège. This is where the likes of Paolo Bettini and Peter
Sagan can flourish, but the *puncheur's puncheur* is probably Philippe Gilbert. In
2011, he became only the second rider to make a clean sweep of all three
Ardennes titles in the same year.

FLAHUTE (FR)

Flanders is to cycling in the same way that South Wales is to rugby or Copacabana
is to football. The northern region of Belgium is not quite as sunny as a Brazilian
beach, perhaps, and the local weather and terrain have helped create a particular

type of cyclist. They're sometimes called Klassikiers – cyclists who are successful in the one-day races not through any particular riding style, but through a sheer toughness in coping with whatever the elements can throw at them.

Indeed, style is something a flahute is almost singular in lacking. A French word to describe a Flandrien cyclist that is believed to have its origins after the Second World War, the term was defined by Harry Pearson in *The Beast, The Emperor and The Milkman* in his own inimitable manner: 'whenever I hear it, something about the sound brings to mind the image of a Tynedale Chimney ... the two things share many characteristics: both are squarely built, sharp-edged and functional to the point of grimness, devoid of any pretension to prettiness.'

Classic flahutes include double world champion 'Iron' Briek Schotte, who according to legend had brown ale in his water bottle and beef stew in his feedbag. Walter Godefroot (nickname 'The Bulldog') had a boxer's nose to go with his Flandrien physique, and was hailed by Eddy Merckx as 'the only one of my adversaries who I never beat in a direct fight for victory.' Freddy 'The Ogre' Maertens was captured by Harry Pearson as 'mighty, powerful, ungainly. He had the big meaty face of John Belushi and his brusqueness marked him out even in the rough and ready world of Flemish cycling.'

Johan Museeuw enjoys the slightly more flattering nickname of 'The Lion of Flanders'. It was a title well deserved given that he won both the Tour of Flanders and Paris-Roubaix three times, and finished on the podium of the former a remarkable eight times in all. At the 1998 Paris-Roubaix, Museeuw crashed on the Trouée d'Arenberg cobbles, smashing up his kneecap and almost losing his leg to a subsequent gangrene infection. He somehow recovered to finish ninth the following year and win the race again in 2000, crossing the finish line by pointedly pointing at his recovered knee. That's a flahute.

ROUTIER-SPRINTEUR (FR)
Velocista (It)

The fast ones. Those remarkable athletes who, despite being knackered having cycled for 200 kilometres, can somehow find it in themselves to produce a devastating burst of speed and win the stage. They're at the front of the race for less that a couple of

hundred metres, but it's the right couple of hundred metres to be at the front.

What sprinters need is described brilliantly by Lionel Birnie in *Zen and the Art of Grand Tour Sprinting*: 'What counts is the make-up of the muscles, or as Cavendish puts it, the perfect balance between fast- and slow-twitch muscle fibres. Slow-twitch fibres contract slowly but can keep going for a long time so are good for endurance.... Fast-twitch fibres contract quickly but tire quickly too. That's where the speed comes from.' A *routier-sprinter* – a road sprinter, rather than a track sprinter – needs twitching muscles aplenty to get through the stage and then compete for the win.

As well as fibres, a large pair of *cojones* don't go amiss either. A bunch sprint is not for the faint-hearted. One false move and you end up like Djamolidine Abdoujaparov on the Champs-Élysées (he crashed with the finish line in sight in 1991). Sean Kelly described the sprint finishes in his days as being like the Wild West: punching, shirt-pulling, whatever it took to get you the win. One tactic to gain those all important milliseconds is 'throwing your bike' – at the right split-second, thrusting your arms forwards and backside out behind the saddle, as Peter Sagan did win his third World Title in Bergen in 2017. Sometimes sprinters will try throwing other things to gain an advantage. At the 1997 Tour, Tom Steels was disqualified for throwing a water bottle at Frederic Moncassin during the stage 6 sprint. Moncassin seemed to be a magnet for attacks that day, with Erik Zabel demoted to last place for head-butting him during the same run-in.

All of that leads to the sprinter often being the showman of the tour – or in Mario Cipollini's case at least until the mountains appeared, at which point he got off his bike and went home. Cipollini cycled with a picture of Pamela Anderson on his handlebars for encouragement and was regularly fined for wearing the wrong colour shorts and jerseys. At the 1999 Tour, his team wore silver jerseys emblazoned with *Veni, Vidi, Vici* (I came, I saw, I conquered) to celebrate his multiple stage wins.

QHUBEKA (NGUNI)

One final group of riders are those that for much of cycling history have been absent from the peloton: That of black and Asian riders.

Cycling, from its earliest origins, has not been the most diverse of sports at the highest level. It's not alone among sports in that, but has perhaps been one of the slowest to rectify this. It was not until 2011 that Guadaloupian Yohann Gène became the first black rider to race in the Tour de France: four years later, Eritrean Daniel Teklehaimanot became the first African rider to wear the King of the Mountains jersey in the competition. Riders from Asia have also been similarly thin on the ground: in 2009, Yukiya Arashiro and Fumiyuki

Beppu became the first Japanese riders to complete the Tour (Kisso Kawamuro in 1926 and Daisuke Imanaka in 1996 had both started but not finished the race); in 2014, Ji Cheng became the first Chinese rider to take part in the Tour.

In the UK, diversity is an issue not just at the top of sport but all the way down: one recent survey showed that while BAME groups make up 41% of the London population, they account for just 7% of its cyclists. A 2019 report, Diversity in Cycling, showed how many cycling clubs are also predominantly white. The report highlighted the work of pioneering groups such as Black Cyclists Network, Brothers on Bikes and the Women of Colour Cycling Group to change this. The report also discussed the example of Team der Ver CC, a club founded by Maurice Burton, the only black professional cyclist in the UK in the late 1970s and early 1980s: Team der Ver has over 60 members, of which half are BAME and a third are female.

In Africa, there are countries where cycling has taken hold and flourished: Eritrea is a good example of this. The country's time as an Italian colony left it with a love of cycling: today, it boasts over 200 professional cyclists, and the Tour de France is shown each year in full on national television. Tim Lewis' fascinating book *Land of Second Chances*, meanwhile, charts the rise and rise of cycling in Rwanda.

One of the biggest forces for change on the continent is Qhubeka, which in 2005 was set up with the aim of helping schoolchildren in poorer communities . Qhubeka is a Ngoni word mean 'to progress' or 'move forwards'. The charity saw a lack of personal transport was one of the major factors in holding children back, and started a programme of distributing bicycles to counter this: by October 2019, the foundation had given away over 100,000 bikes.

At the same time, Qhubeka became involved in professional cycling, partly to help promote their work. This led to the foundation of the MTN Qhubeka team (later Dimension Data for Qhubeka and NTT Pro Cycling). In 2015, MTN Qhubeka became the first African-registered team to take part in the Tour de France and in 2016 the first African team to be awarded a UCI World Tour license. Part of Dimension Data's 'Vision 2020' goal was to win the Tour de France with an African rider by 2020.

Instead, the 2020 Tour saw just one black rider in the peloton – Kevin Reza, riding for B&B Hotels-Vital Concept. And while other sports reacted strongly to the appalling death of George Floyd and the resulting Black Lives Matters protests, the response in cycling was noticeably more muted: the Tour's belated gesture was cyclists wearing masks at the start of the final stage, with 'End Racism' written on in marker.

FOUR | The Season

The cycling calendar is one that begins in early spring and ends in the autumn. Over those nine months or so the sport takes in all sorts of different terrains and types of race, from three-week Grand Tours to one-day Classics. What follows is by no means an exhaustive list, but a whistle-stop through the highlights of the season.

THE CLASSICS

A Classic is a one-day race. They take place predominantly, but not always, in the early part of the season and mostly, but not always, in Belgium and northern France. Quite what constitutes a 'Classic' is a slightly grey area – it's usually to do with age and prestige, though the Amstel Gold has only been going since the late 1960s; the San Sebastian started in the early 1980s, and the Strade Bianche was first held in 2007.

But these are the exceptions; most of the Classics have been an established part of the cycling calendar for many decades. We're talking races with wonderfully evocative names like Omloop Het Nieuswblad, Het Volk, Ghent–Wevelgem, Flèche Wallonne, Scheldeprijs, and Dwars Door Vlandeeren. Not all Classics have made it through to the present day. The Bordeaux–Paris race that Jacques Anquetil famously won in 1965 straight after winning the Dauphiné, shut up shop in 1988. World wars couldn't stop the Championship of Zurich, but a twentieth-century lack of sponsorship did. The ones that survive and thrive take the riders through every terrain imaginable – climbs, flats, gravel, cobbles – whatever the type of cyclist, there's a Classic with their name on it. Compared

to the team-dominated Tours, the one-day winner-takes-all feel adds an additional frisson of excitement to Classics season, a flash of the unexpected, and a level of devotion from real cycling connoisseurs everywhere.

THE MONUMENTS

Some Classics are bigger than others and five in particular have become the most coveted one-day events to have on your *palmarés* (*see* Chapter Five): Milan–San Remo, The Tour of Flanders, Paris–Roubaix, Liège–Bastogne–Liège and the Tour of Lombardy. These have become known collectively as the 'Monuments'; a relatively recent term that merely confirms their already legendary status.

In fact, their pre-eminence among the top-tier of Classics has long been apparent. In a forerunner of the present-day UCI World Tour, the Challenge Desgrange–Colombo was a year-long cycling competition where riders accumulated points from their position in different races. Alongside the Tour de France and Giro, all five Monuments featured, alongside a smattering of other races, including Paris–Brussels and the Tour de Suisse. Fast forward to the present day and the UCI World Tour now follows a similar set-up. In terms of world ranking points, the five Monuments are the highest scoring one-day events and on a par with all the major stage-races, with the exception of the Grand Tours.

MILAN–SAN REMO
La Classicissima di Primavera /The Spring Classic

The first Monument of the season, La Classicissima di Primavera begins in the might of industrial Milan and ends in San Remo, a seaside town that set up the race to counteract its image as a fading resort best known for gambling – a sort of Great Yarmouth but with better weather. The one-day race was in fact the second attempt to set up a Milan–San Remo event. The first try was as a car rally, but only two of the vehicles entered actually made it to the finish. Not that the early versions of the cycling Classic went much better. In 1910, horrendous weather saw only a handful of riders reach the end. The eventual winner, Eugène Christophe, had to take shelter in an inn to warm up half way through, spent the next month in hospital recovering from frostbite and took two years to fully recover.

It doesn't always snow at Milan-San Remo and even when it does, the route gets altered these days; in 2013, 50 kilometres were chopped out because of snow and sub-zero temperatures. Organizers have tried to harden up the route over the years with the addition of climbs over the Poggio (1960) and Cipressa (1982) to counteract the race's reputation as a sprinter's classic. The Poggio (which means 'little hill') isn't the high point of the race by any means, but its position six kilometres from the finish can be a crucial moment in the race. In 1992, Moreno Argentin seemed assured of victory, until Sean Kelly pulled off one of the great descents on the Poggio to catch him. But stay in contention over the Poggio and a sprinter is in with a shout of victory; Mario Cippolini, Alessandro Petacchi and Erik Zabel have all emerged triumphant over the last few decades. Zabel, who won the Mounument four times between 1997 and 2001, would have had a fifth title in 2004 had Óscar Freire not snuck past as he was celebrating.

TOUR OF FLANDERS
Vlaanderens Mooiste ('Flanders' Finest')/De Ronde van Vlaanderen / De Ronde (Fl)

'You have left, you have right, you have down, you have up, you have climbs with cobbles, climbs without cobbles, you have everything.' So says Fabian Cancellera, winner of Vlaanderens Mooiste in 2010, 2013 and 2014. The combination of Flanders and bikes is a bit like Wales and rugby – the passion the locals have for the sport is all-consuming and fiercely local. Eddy Merckx might have been the greatest cyclist that Belgium, and indeed the world, has ever produced but he was from Brussels and spoke French, so wasn't a patch on Rik Van Looy, Freddy Maartens, Roger de Vlaeminck or Johan Museeuw if you're from Flanders. And in 1976 he even had the ignominy of having to get off and push his bike up the slopes of the Koppenberg. Those fancy Brussels ways won't help him here...

To be fair to Merckx, there were another 162 riders doing the same. The Koppenberg was the latest of the race's cobbled *hellingen* (Dutch for hills). It's only 600 metres long but has a 25 per cent kick to it. In that first year it was included in the race, only five riders managed to get over it on their bikes: 'You might as well make the cyclists climb ladders with bikes around their necks', Merckx complained, but the climb has been a fans' favourite ever since. When a local newspaper ran an April Fools Day story in 1997 that the Koppenberg was about to be tarmacked over, a thousand people turned up to protest.

Other famous climbs in the race include Oude Kwaremont near the beginning, Paterburg (purpose built by a local farmer in the 1980s) and the Kapelmuur (Chapel Wall) at Geraardsbergen. The latter was dropped from the race in 2011 to howls of protest and a mock funeral involving masked lycra-clad men carrying a

Above Beaten by the Koppenberg at
the 1985 Tour of Flanders

coffin. The Muur had long been a decisive part of the race – the local saying was that 'The Wall shall choose the winner.' Which might sound a bit *Game of Thrones* but such is the severity of de Ronde that it is a race where legends are born.

KERMESSE (FL)
Also *Kermis* (Dutch)

'Like a local crit race on crack', as one participant put it, *kermesses* are Flemish and Dutch circuit races that take place as part of a local festival (the name comes from 'church' and 'mass'). The race circuits are longer than a criterium (five to ten kilometres) and the race itself longer too – two to three hours rather than an hour and half.

And while the criterium circuit can have an air of exhibition about it (*see* below), *kermesses* are hard-fought races right from the off. The first half hour can often be a flat-out affair, knackering everyone before breakaways start forming in the second. They are often ruled over by the 'Lords of the Kermesse', older riders with a lot of racing know-how and legs covered in embrocation.

With their bursts of cobbles and their full-throttle racing, their demand for both brilliant bike handling and tactical acumen, they are the perfect training ground for the spring Classics, and an important factor behind the Belgian dominance of these races for so many years.

PARIS–ROUBAIX
L'enfer du Nord ('The Hell of the North') (Fr)/*La Pascale* ('The Easter Race') (Fr)

Stage races have an *étape reine* – the queen stage – which is usually the highest, the longest, the hardest, or all three put together. The spring Classics have *La Reine* – the Queen of the Classics in the form of Paris–Roubaix.

When the idea of Paris–Roubaix first evolved in the 1890s, it wasn't even a race in its own right. The original plan of the race organizers was that it would be a warm up for the much longer and already established Bordeaux–Paris: Paris–Roubaix would be a 'training race' and its 280 kilometres 'child's play' compared to the longer event.

Not many people have called Paris–Roubaix 'child's play' since then. Its popular nickname, *L'enfer du Nord* (The Hell of the North), doesn't actually come from a description of the race, but from an article by journalist Victor Breyer surveying the landscape in the aftermath of the First World War. Such is the harshness of the race, the name has stuck.

Paris–Roubaix isn't a hilly route. But it has cobbles. Lots of them. Section after section of narrow bone-shaking road, once famously described by Steve Bauer as 'like sitting on a pneumatic drill.' Not everyone is a fan: Bernard Hinault proclaimed, 'This isn't a race, it's cyclo-cross... Paris–Roubaix is bullshit.' Certainly, it's a race that requires bravery and concentration. If you don't hit the *pavé* sections at the front, you risk getting stuck behind a crash. If it's a dry day, then you're going to get covered and choked by dust. And if it's a wet day, then the cobbles are lethal. (Just to rub it in, the trophy for winning the race is not your usual gold-encrusted dinner plate or cup, but an *actual sodding cobblestone*).

More than any other Classic, this is the race that riders want to win. Jacques Goddet once called it 'the last test of folly that cycle sport puts before its participants', but any cyclist with an understanding of tradition dreams of entering the Roubaix velodrome out in front. It was the race that Bradley Wiggins, always a rider with a keen sense of cycling history, chose to end his road career on – attacking off the front with four kilometres to go, he eventually finished eighteenth. Perhaps Paris–Roubaix is best summed up by the Dutch rider Theo de Rooij, who abandoned the race in 1985 after five draining hours at the front. Interviewed afterwards, his spat

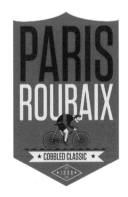

out, 'It's bollocks this race! You work like an animal, you don't have time to piss, you wet your pants. You're riding in mud like this, you're slipping, it's a piece of shit...' Will you ever ride it again? The interviewer asked. 'Of course, de Rooij replies, 'it's the most beautiful race in the world.'

LIÈGE–BASTOGNE–LIÈGE
La Doyenne ('The Old Lady') (Fr)

As the name suggests, La Doyenne is the oldest of the Monuments – and pretty much the oldest race on the cycling calendar (Milan–Turin began earlier, but has not been raced as many times). Like Paris–Roubaix, the race started as a precursor to a longer event, in this instance the now defunct Paris–Brest–Paris. The organizers had a vision of a Liège–Paris–Liège spectacular and in 1892 ran a test Liège–Bastogne–Liège event. Bastogne was chosen because officials could get there and back by train in a day.

The longer event never happened but La Doyenne quickly took hold as a popular fixture. For a while it vied with the younger La Flèche Wallonne for

Below Hell for cyclists, heaven for cycling fans. Tackling the *pavé* at the 1968 Paris–Roubaix

dominance: in the 1950s, the two races were run as a weekend double-header on successive days, but La Doyenne emerged the stronger and these days forms the climax of Ardennes Week – Amstel Gold running the weekend before and *La Flèche Wallonne* slotting in midweek.

The race route doesn't have anything quite as steep as the Koppenberg or the Mur du Hoy but still has plenty of famous hills, such as La Redoute and the Stockeu, for riders to contend with. The sheer relentlessness of the climbs means that it is the strongest rather than the smartest rider who usually comes out on top. 'What matters in Liège is pure physical strength,' claims double-winner Michele Bartoli. 'Tactics count for much less.'

When the weather takes a turn for the worse, this 'hard man' aspect comes to the fore. Such were the blizzard conditions of the 1980 edition that the race became known as Neige–Bastogne–Neige (*see* Chapter Fourteen). An early snowstorm took out two-thirds of the 175 starters, with Bernard Hinault eventually leading home the forty-odd riders who made it to the finish, winning by nine minutes. His victory came at a cost: he had no feeling in his hands for weeks afterwards and his fingers are still sensitive to the cold today.

THE GRAND TOURS

Just as the Monuments are the pick of the Classics, so the three Grand Tours of cycling are the cream of the stage races. The three events – the Giro d'Italia, the Tour de France and the Vuelta a España – are the longest stage races on the calendar, each clocking in at three weeks, with only a couple of rest days for respite. For those who care about these things, their prestige is reflected in the world ranking points on offer: 200 for the Tour winner and 170 for the Giro/Vuelta (with no other event awarding more than 100 points).

Most riders, though, are only interested in the history of being a Grand Tour winner. Like the majors in tennis and golf, these are the events that every rider dreams of having on their *palmarès* (*see* Chapter Five). Just as only five golfers and seven tennis players have ever achieved a 'career grand slam' (winning all four major titles), so only seven riders have ever achieved the cycling equivalent of winning all three Grand Tours: Jacques Anquetil, Alberto Contador, Chris Froome, Felice Gimondi, Bernard Hinault, Eddy Merckx and Vincenzo Nibali.

The term 'Grand Tour' originated a few hundred years earlier, to describe the vogue for well-to-do young men to embark on an educational rites of passage excursion around the historical and cultural highlights of Europe. It's a concept that is echoed in the Grand Tour races today: just swap travelling on horseback for travelling by bike, seeing the artworks of Titian for the slopes of the Tourmalet, and replace an invigorating box of snuff with a syringeful of EPO.

THE GIRO
La Giro d'Italia (It)/*La Corsa Rosa* ('The Pink Route') (It)

The first Grand Tour of the year, the Giro d'Italia, was set up at the start of the twentieth century in the wake of the success of the Tour de France. As with the Tour, the driving force was a newspaper, in this case *La Gazzetta dello Sport*. *La Gazzetta* was already behind the one-day Classic Milan–San Remo and the Tour of Lombardy, but made the move into setting up a stage race to pre-empt the plans of rival newspaper *Il Corriere della Sera*. The leader's pink jersey comes from the colour of the paper that *La Gazzetta* is printed on, though the *maglia rosa* (*see* Chapter Five) wasn't introduced until 1931.

The first race took place in 1909, setting off from Milan at just before 3 am. Stages were long (up to 400 kilometres) and the original cyclists weren't helped by the fact that bikes didn't have any gears. The winner was a bricklayer, Luigi Ganna, though the race was decided under a points rather than a time system (in modern GC terms, he'd have only just scraped onto the podium). Asked how he felt on winning the race, his answer was simple: 'My arse is killing me.'

Three factors gives the Giro its distinctive feel compared to the other Grand Tours. Firstly, there's the weather: as the earliest race in the season, in late May, riders often have to contend with snow up in the mountains. Andy Hampsten (1998) and Nairo Quintana (2013) both cemented their dominance of the race in blizzard conditions. Secondly, there are the *tifosi* (*see* Chapter Eight) – the passionate and partisan fans who cheer and chastise the riders up the mountainsides. When Stephen Roche won the 1987 Giro at the expense of his team leader Roberto Visentini, the crowds punched him and shouted 'bastardo!', waved raw meat at him and daubed his *maglia rosa* in red wine. Thirdly, there's the sheer *Italianness* of proceedings. It wasn't until the 1950s that a non-Italian won the race and thus many of the race's myths and legends – Binda, Guerra, Bartali, Coppi – are an all-Italian affair.

The difficulty of riding both the Giro and the Tour in the same year forces most riders to choose one or the other in a single season: many non-Italian riders thus prioritise the Tour as the bigger race. Lance Armstrong did not ride the Giro until his comeback in 2009; Chris Froome, disqualified from the 2010 race for holding on to a motorbike, did not race the Giro again until he won it in 2018. Yet the dominance of the Tour as the pre-eminent race is a fairly recent phenomenon. For many years, the Giro more than held its own and those with an understanding of cycling history know the importance of having the Giro on your *palmarés*: following his success at the 2012 Tour, for example, Bradley Wiggins tried and failed to add the pink jersey to his trophy cabinet.

What hasn't been achieved in nearly 20 years is the Giro–Tour double. In 1998, Marco Pantani became the last of only seven riders to manage it and there is a question as to whether the demands of modern cycling now make this achievement impossible (indeed, there is a question as to whether Pantani's own success was completely legitimate, as he was disqualified from the race the following year). Alberto Contador attempted the double in 2015, winning the Giro but looking exhausted in the Tour, finishing a distant fifth.

One other historical footnote: the Giro D'Italia is the only one of the three Grand Tours ever to feature a female rider. In 1924, Alfonisna Strada was secretly invited to take part and signed in as 'Alfonsin', her identity only discovered once the race had got underway. The Giro of the time was brutal, consisting of twelve stages at an average length of 300 km. As dozens of riders abandoned the race, Strada cycled on: each day she was finishing towards the back of the field, but the *tifosi* would wait hours to cheer her on. On the stage from L'Aquila to Perugia, Strada crashed badly, breaking her handlebars in the process. Following an impromptu fix with a broom handle, she eventually crossed the finishing line well beyond the time limit. Such was her popularity, the organisers paid for her to continue anyway. Strada made it to the end in Milan, which was more than two-thirds of the riders at the start managed to achieve.

GIRO ROSA (IT)
Giro D'Italia Femminile (formerly *Giro Donne*)

While in male cycling it has been the Tour de France that has outpaced the Giro, in women's cycling, it is the Italian race that has grown to become the pre-eminent Grand Tour.

It was the French who struck first when the Tour de France Féminin was launched in 1984. The route echoed that of the men's Tour, using the same roads but starting further up the course to make the stages shorter, and with the women racing earlier in the day. The race was won by Marianne Martin, with her American team adding the team prize and the polka dot jersey to her own *maillot jaune* (*see* Chapter Five). But the race has faced difficulties over the years: copyright problems over the name led to it being renamed the clunky Grande Boucle Féminin Internationale in the late 1990s. Rather than echoing the Tour route, the race shed stages left, right and centre, – from 21 in 1984 to fifteen, down to ten and just four in 2009. The race was cancelled after that and: the following year, the other longstanding French stage race, the Tour de L'Aude Cycliste Féminin, was also stopped. This left the six-stage Route de France Féminin as the last race standing, but the last iteration of this was held in 2016. Since 2014, the Tour de France have held the clumsily titled La Course by the Tour de France, but with the exception of 2017, this has been a single stage race (the 2017 edition had two stages).

The Giro D'Italia Feminille, by contrast, may have started later (it's inaugural race in 1988 was won by Maria Canins) but has grown to be both the pre-eminent, and now the only, women's Grand Tour. Taking place in late June and early July, it typically runs over ten stages. Matching the achievements of Binda, Coppi and Merckx, the Italian cyclist Fabiana Luperini has won the female Giro five times, including four years straight in the mid 1990s: more recently, the race has been dominated by the Dutch with wins for Marianne Vos (2011, 2012 and 2014), Anna van der Breggen (2015 and 2017) and Annemiek van Vleuten (2018 and 2019).

The Giro Rosa might not have as many stages as La Corsa Rosa, but its route usually packs a similar punch. The 2016 edition took the riders up the slopes of the Mortirolo, for example. Even so, not everyone is completely au fait as yet with its importance. In an interview in spring 2016, Emma Pooley made the not unreasonable observation that while money had been poured into helping a British rider win the Tour de France, she'd finished second in the *Giro Rosa* in the same period, but with no assistance forthcoming to help her up that extra step on the podium. Team Sky rider Peter Kennaugh responded on Twitter, asking, 'why would Sky put money into women's giro that absolutely no-one in the UK has absolutely no idea about?', endearing himself further by adding, 'stop being so self-centred and get over it.' Twitter, unsurprisingly, begged to differ.

CRITÉRIUM DU DAUPHINÉ
(formerly *Critérium du Dauphiné Libéré*) (Fr)

The Queen's Tournament to the Tour's Wimbledon, the *Critérium du Dauphiné* is the pick of the warm-up events before the biggest race on the cycling calendar. Although the Tour de Suisse and the Route du Sud have their champions, the *Critérium* has featured the winner of every Tour de France for the last decade, bar 2010 (when Alberto Contador's disqualification handed the Tour title to Andy Schleck) and 2019 (Egan Bernal ending up as co-leader for the Tour after Chris Froome's crash during that year's *Critérium*).

The week-long race was first staged in 1947 at the behest of the *Dauphiné Libéré* newspaper. It was originally set up to celebrate the demilitarisation of the Alps following the end of the Second World War and boost the newspaper's circulation in the process (the paper's name also comes from the region's liberation). Dauphiné is a region in the south-east of France and home to such Tour favourites as Ventoux and the Galibier. The race offers riders a Tour de France in miniature, with a time-trial and a couple of Alpine mountain stages on which to test themselves out. As for the region's name, the dolphin link (Dauphin is French for dolphin) can be traced back to the twelfth century, when local ruler Count Guiges IV had dolphins on his coat of arms to designate that he was well-travelled.

Back in the day, *dauphin* was also the title given to the heir apparent to the French throne; you know, before the revolution and all that whatnot. So it's kind of a fitting name for a warm-up event for the Tour. Bradley Wiggins, Chris Froome and Geraint Thomas all preceded Tour wins with victory in the *Dauphiné*, cementing their position with the bookmakers as favourite for the longer race.

But although the Tour winner has tended to take part in the *Dauphiné*, by no means do they always win it. In 2014, Vincenzo Nibali looked well off the pace and a completely different rider to the one who would go on to dominate the Tour. In *The Rider,* David Millar argues that the Wiggins/Froome wins are the exception rather the norm: 'the final results don't carry much relevance regarding performance at the Tour – to the point that it's often said that if you have a good *Dauphiné*, you're likely to have a bad Tour and a bad *Dauphiné* means a good Tour.' History appears to bear Millar out: the first winner of the *Dauphiné*, Edouard Klabinski, finished 34th in that year's Tour; the most recent winner, Jakob Fuglsang, did not finish the 2019 Tour (he also did the *Dauphiné*/ DNF double in 2017 as well). In total, only fourteen times out of 71 *Dauphinés* has the winner gone on to win the Tour – and that number is only if you include Lance Armstrong's victories. A bit like the curse of the Rainbow Jersey (see later), the *Dauphiné* as Tour guide is a bit of a cycling myth.

THE TOUR DE FRANCE
La Grande Boucle ('The Great Loop') (Fr)

The one even your gran has heard about. For the non-aficionado the Tour de France *is* cycling, in the same way that the tennis season is a Wimbledon fortnight and American Football is a one-off game that serves as a warm-up act to promote Beyoncé's new single. It's the one we all started watching first.

Today, the Tour is huge. ASO, the organization behind the Tour, proudly proclaim it to be the third biggest sporting event on the planet after the Olympics and the World Cup, and the largest annual one. It gets a global television audience of 3.5 billion and is broadcast to 188 countries. On top of which, is the spectacle itself. An average of twelve million fans line the route, a number topped up when the race makes one of its *Grand Départs* in a different country. When the Tour came to the UK in 2014, it is estimated that 3.5 million turned out to watch the race, including 2.3 million in Yorkshire, where the race started – about one in four of the population of God's Own County.

Above Jean Canova taking on a snowy Col du Galibier at the 1925 Tour de France

The Tour de France was the brainchild of Henri Desgrange, editor of the *L'Auto*, a newspaper – ironically enough given the on-going animosity between riders and motorists – that was about cars, first and foremost, with other sports a secondary concern. Desgrange was looking for a way to boost the newspaper in its fight for circulation with rival publication *Vélo* and hit upon the idea of a cycling race. In his history of the Tour de France, *Le Tour*, Geoffrey Wheatcroft cites a classic children's schoolbook, *Tour de France par Deux Enfants*, in which two young brothers go on a sojourn in France following the death of their father. The book was published in 1877 and by 1900 had sold six million copies. For a whole generation, the idea of a journey around the *hexagone* was already embedded in the culture: Desgrange took the concept and established it as a cycling race.

'With the grand and powerful gesture that Zola gave his working man in *La Terre*, *L'Auto*, newspaper of ideas and action, will from today send across France

those unconscious and hardy sowers of energy, the professional road racer.' Thus declared Desgrange in a newspaper editorial in July 1903. There were 60 hardy sowers of energy in that first race, with 21 making it through to the finish. At first glance, the race wasn't dissimilar to a modern Tour, being three weeks long and just under 2500 kilometres in length. The difference was that these kilometres were divided into six monster stages with lots of rest in between. The longest stage was the opening 467 kilometres, taking the riders through the night and then some, from Paris to Lyon: the race was won by Maurice Gaurin, nicknamed 'le petit ramoneur' because he was, well, *petit* and a *ramoneur* (chimney sweep).

As with anything that becomes too large and successful, there's always the danger that the long-standing fans get a bit dismissive now everyone else likes what only they used to know about. It's a bit like the difference between between being a U2 fan in 1983 and one in 2003. To sell out stadiums, to appeal to a wide audience, some of the edges that make a band interesting get rubbed off in the process. The Coldplay effect, if you will. The blander, broader brush strokes might annoy the cognoscenti – if you can imagine such a thing as a Coldplay cognoscenti – but that smoothing out is integral to international success. It's a challenge that faces any major sporting event. There was a similar debate over the football World Cup in 2014 – whether the competition had got too big and corporate to really excite. Was the World Cup better back in the day, or did we just remember it that way because we were younger and experiencing it for the first time?

Has the Tour to some degree become a victim of its remarkable success? Such is its size that it needs roads of a certain magnitude through which to hawk its publicity *caravane* (*see* Chapter 8) – ruling out some of the narrower climbs, say, of the Vuelta. It was highly unusual for the Tour to go up a climb like the Lacets de Montvernier in 2015, where accompanying cars had to be redirected and fans banned from the roadside. Then there is the question of familiarity: while the Vuelta continues to add new climbs to its ranks, the Tour isn't the Tour unless it climbs the likes of the Tourmalet, Ventoux, the Galibier or Alpe d'Huez. Not that these climbs aren't brilliant, but their presence is about the history of the race, rather than bringing in something new.

Whisper it very quietly, but sometimes the Tour can be a bit, well, *dull* in comparison to the other Grand Tours. The 2014 race, when Nibali won at a canter after Froome and Contador withdrew, was over as a contest about a third of the race in. The 2012 race, a bit like the 1966 World Cup, was brilliant if you were English, but less so for the rest of the world. One could blame the tactics of Team Sky here – their stifling strategy of getting the race lead and then riding a relentlessly high tempo to stop anyone attacking. One could blame Lance Armstrong (among various things you could blame Lance Armstrong for) for biding his time in the opening week then winning big on the first mountain stage and effectively neutering the race from thereon in. One could blame Big Mig – Miguel Indurain's relentless five tour wins gained by blitzing the time-trial and holding on in the mountains.

But follow this chronological argument through and it could be argued that the last time the Tour was properly and consistently brilliant was in the mid- to late 1980s, when Greg LeMond pipped Laurent Fignon on the Champs-Élysées by eight seconds, when Bernard Hinault belligerently battled it out with the rider he was meant to be supporting, and when Stephen Roche went *mano-a-mano* with Pedro Delgado.

In the last few Tours, there are signs that the organisers are at least trying to rectify this and cancel out the benefits of the teams with the largest budgets. In 2018, they trialled a grand prix style start for one stage, which at 65 km was also the shortest stage in recent memory, in the hope of shaking things up (it didn't). The 2019 route tried to favour the pure climbers, with seven summits over 2000 metres and just 27.2 individual time-trial kilometres (this time, the weather got in the way, with the key mountain stage abandoned). When the 2020 route was announced, with the first mountain stage on the second day, and the only (also mountainous) time-trial on the second last day, Chris Froome described it as 'the hardest route I've seen anywhere in the past five years,' while race director Christian Prudhomme described it as one with 'traps everywhere'.

So maybe the Tour is still the greatest race on earth. Maybe if you're thirteen years old and settling down to watch Pogacar and Bernal and Dumoulin and Roglic for the first time, you're doing so with the same wide-eyed enthusiasm as fans in the 1980s. The Tour is the first bite of the cycling bug, and properly bitten, it'll remain with you for life.

THE CRITERIUMS

Criteriums – sometimes known as 'crits' – are circuit-based races, often around a provincial town centre. The circuits and race lengths tend to be shorter than the Flemish *kermesses* (*see* above) and although they take place at various times and in various countries, they are usually run in France, Belgium and the Netherlands in the aftermath of the Tour.

Criteriums are an opportunity for fans to see the big names of the Tour at first hand – and the big names of the Tour to cash in with appearance fees. That was a big deal when prize money and salaries weren't what they are today. The money for a personal appearance is not to be sneezed at: Jan Ullrich could command £15-20,000 in the late 1990s. Then there are the *primes* – the prizes, which are divvied up in agreement between the main riders in advance of the race. This can lead to odd spectacles, such as Greg Van Avermaet and Vincenzo Nibali outsprinting Marcel Kittel at the 2015 Criterium Aalst.

Occasionally a rider doesn't play ball with what has been agreed. At the 1975 Circuit de l'Aulne Criterium in Châteaulin, a young, newly turned professional Bernard Hinault was kept out of the 'pool' of who would share the *primes* agreed between the established riders. 'Watch me', he said to one fellow rider, going on to beat Eddy Merckx to the first three *primes*; at which point Merckx told him if he calmed down, he could be in on the deal with the other riders; at which point Hinault did no such thing and won the next *prime* too. It was quite the statement of intent.

THE VUELTA
Vuelta a España (Sp)/*Vuelta Ciclista a España* (Sp)

The least grand of the three Grand Tours, the Vuelta is also by far the youngest. It began in April 1935 at the behest of another newspaper interested in boosting its circulation: in this case the Madrid paper *Informaciones* and its director, Juan

Pujol. The Vuelta wasn't the first attempt to set up a Spanish race. Attempts had been made two decades earlier by the Barcelona paper *El Mundo Deportivo*, but foundered thanks to the competing politics of Madrid and Catalonia. Ironically, it was politics that later helped get the Vuelta off the ground: one of the driving forces behind the race was former cyclist Clemente López Dóriga, who had Nationalist intentions behind his vision.

National politics certainly influenced the early part of the Vuelta's history. Spain's pariah status under Franco proved a challenge in establishing the race – organizers would pay 'starting money' and design routes in the hope of appealing to big names: a nice long time-trial for Jacques Anquetil here, some sprinter-friendly stages for Rik van Looy. Then there was the timing of the race. With the Giro and the Tour already firmly established, the Vuelta was originally an early season affair in late April/early May, making for a very concentrated Grand Tour season. This meant that many big names skipped the Vuelta; Miguel Indurain, for example, preferred to ride the Giro in preparation for the Tour. Thirdly, the Vuelta lacked an Alps or a Pyrenees or a Dolomites to draw in the climbers: 'Spain doesn't have enough mountains to decide a race', claimed the organizers, with race director Luis Bergareche telling critics, 'I can't bring the Tourmalet to Spain.'

Today, the Vuelta is a different beast. It's now the last Grand Tour on the calendar, run from the end of August into September since its shift in 1995. That creates a different dynamic among its participants. While cyclists tend to opt for either the Giro or the Tour, doubling up with the Vuelta is a far more practical possibility – Giro riders benefitting from the break between races, Tour riders able to continue any form built up in that race. Then there are the riders whose season, for whatever reason (injury or whatever), hasn't worked out the way they hoped: the Vuelta gives them one final shot at glory to redeem their year.

The Vuelta has also added an ever-widening selection of mountains into its stage route. It took until 1972 for the Vuelta to have a mountain-top finish: in 2015, the race had a whole host of them. Today it's the sprinters rather than the climbers who gripe about the route. 'The Vuelta has just become stupid now,' Mark Cavendish complained in 2015. 'Eleven mountain-top finishes this year... sprinters aren't bad bike riders. You don't have to go quick uphill to make it a good race, do you know what I mean?'

Yet for all Cavendish's protestations, it is the hills that have made the Vuelta often the most interesting race of the three Grand Tours. The organizers have added new mountains to the route, most famously the Angliru, which made its debut in 1999: it has an average gradient of 13 per cent over the last six kilometres, with some sections having a whopping 24 per cent. When David Millar rode up it in 2002, such was the severity of the slope that he 'had to weave through broken-down cars and the dark misty air stank of burned-out clutches' (furious at the difficulty of the day, he tore his number off and walked over the finish line). Nine years later, Bradley Wiggins came to a virtual standstill on the Angliru, losing the leader's red jersey to the eventual winner Juan Jose Cobo. (Cobo in turn, would lose that red jersey in 2019 to runner-up Chris Froome, when he was stripped of his title for anti-doping violations).

Over the last few years, the Vuelta has consistently been the most unpredictable and the most fun of the Grand Tours – the four-way ding dong between Froome, Contador, Valverde and Rodriguez in 2012 and 2014; 41-year-old Chris Horner surprising Nibali in 2013; the battle between Tom Dumolin and Fabio Aru in 2015. Like an older sibling, the Tour might have the greater authority, but it's the younger Vuelta that has more fun.

THE WORLDS

Technically, they're called the UCI Road World Championships. In reality, everyone just calls them the Worlds. They are different races: junior and under-23, men's and women's, time-trial and road, but for some, the only race that matters is the final event – the Elite Men's Road Race.

The Worlds have been held since 1927, when Alfredo Binda won in Nürburgring, Germany. Indeed, such was the domination of the Italians, that Binda's teammates finished second, third and fourth as well. It's a race that the Italians have continued to do well in: their 19 victories only beaten by Belgium's haul of 26, with no other country even getting into double figures. The Belgian and Italian numbers are even more impressive given that no rider has ever won the world title more than three times – its not like there's a Merckx (three times) or

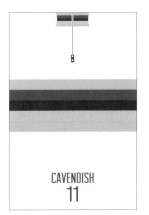

CAVENDISH

11

a Coppi (once) distorting the figures with a massive personal haul.

The race takes place towards the end of the cycling season, after the Vuelta; indeed some riders use the Vuelta (and also the Tour of Britain) to help get them ready for the Worlds. The race is a bit like a one-day Classic in length, except the course usually involves seemingly endless loops around a large circuit. The location is different each year, as is the course, to give different types of rider a chance of winning. Oh, and unlike the rest of the season, the riders find themselves racing for their countries, rather than their professional teams.

Some riders love the event: 'The Worlds is one of my favourite events,' David Millar wrote in *The Rider*. 'It has an energy about it like no other... it's the only time in the year we get to race for our country, which means different riders, different staff, different team kit. It all feels new, which is something of a tonic by September... for many of us the Worlds will be our final race of the year, which gives it a last-day-of-school buzz.'

Others see the race as more anachronistic. Charly Wegelius in *Domestique* argues that, 'once professional teams were employing riders from twelve different nations, the idea of a World Championships run off in national teams should have become obsolete as allegiences among professionals were always going to be skewed. But it didn't, and so instead the race became what it was: a race that masqueraded as one that was based on national pride, but was in fact as mercenary as any other bike race.' For Wegelius that conflict came to a head at the 1994 Worlds, when as part of the GB team, he put his professional career first by accepting an offer to help the Italian team in the race.

Riding in national teams can promote a coming together of riders – the British supporting Mark Cavendish to victory in 2011, Sean Kelly helping Stephen Roche to complete a 'triple crown' of Giro, Tour and Worlds in 1987 – but it can also expose long simmering rivalries. Such was the enmity between Fausto Coppi and Gino Bartali that when both were selected for the Italian team in 1948, they spent the race making sure that the other person wasn't going to win. Booed off when they withdrew, they were banned for two months as a result.

Mark Cavendish is one of two British men to win the World Title – Tom Simpson being the other in 1965. In the Women's race, the British have won five times: Beryl Burton (twice), followed by Mandy Jones, Nicole Cook and Lizzie Armistead. Marianne Vos, perhaps inevitably, is the most successful modern female – between 2006 and 2013, she won the title three times and finished second a further five times. In the men's race, the nearest example of dominance was by Peter Sagan, who in 2017 became the first male rider to win three titles in a row.

GIRO DI LOMBARDIA (IT)
La Classica della foglie morte ('The Race of the Falling Leaves') (It)/ Il Lombardia (It)

'Italian races are tailored in the same way that Italians like to tailor everything: perfectly designed to get the very best out of the riders and the environment. The race routes take into account what the weather will be doing and where the sunlight will fall. It's no accident that the bookend races of the Italian season – Milan–San Remo and Lombardia – have such beautifully lit finishes: the spring sunlight bathes the finish of the first and the autumn light fades luxuriantly on the last.'

This wonderful description of Italian racing from Charly Wegelius' *Domenstique* captures the essence of what makes The Race of the Falling Leaves one of the most glorious races of the season. The last of the five Monuments, it is held the week after the Worlds, and although there are other lesser events here and there, it is essentially the last word on the cycling season.

The race was first held in 1905 at the behest of *La Gazzetta* newspaper, who chose the late season date to make the race distinctive. The roads might not have been the quality that they are today, but the beauty of the scenery was ever present: the Lombardian lakes and mountains north of Milan, all glistening and golden in the autumnal sunshine. The first winner, Giovanni Gerbi, was less than golden in his tactics. Gerbi used his local knowledge to win the first race, forcing the pace and the unsuspecting peloton to fall onto the tramlines he knew to avoid; in 1907 he was disqualified after he again manouevred himself into the front and his supporters closed a level crossing behind him.

'The Italian races are designed to suit the cunning mind', says Wegelius. 'In Italy it is never enough just to be strong, like it is in Belgium and northern France... in Italy the racing is designed so you have to choose your perfect moment.' That's certainly true with Lombardia: in 2015, Vincenzo Nibali salvaged a miserable season (and a disqualification from the Vuelta for holding on to the back of the team car) with a perfectly timed attack on the descent of the final climb of the Civiglo – a masterclass in going downhill and a quite brilliant solo victory.

The history of the Giro di Lombardia is littered with epic cycling battles and landmarks. The most famous site on the route is the chapel on the Madonna del Ghisallo, overlooking Lake Como below. The chapel has become a shrine for the sport, with Pope Pius XII declaring the Madonna the patroness of cycling in 1949. Now a site of pilgrimage for cyclists, the chapel is such a haven for memorabilia that an adjacent building has had to be built to host it all, including everything from the bike Fausto Coppi used to break the hour record to the largest collection of *maglie rose* in the world.

For all that cycling has changed over the years, there will always be something timeless about the riders of the Lombardia weaving their way up the slopes of the Ghisallo in the autumn sunshine, with the bells of the chapel ringing out to greet them.

FIVE | Prizes

'All must have prizes,' claimed the Dodo in *Alice's Adventures in Wonderland*. It's an argument that cycling begs to differ on, offering its famous rewards to only the very best the sport has to offer. Behold, then, a selection of jerseys (and ribbons) in pretty much every colour of the rainbow, and a rainbow jersey with a colour scheme all of its own...

PALMARÈS (FR/SP)

Cycling for achievements. If a rider was going for a job interview, their *palmarès* is what they'd have on their CV. Quite what you'd put on depends what you've won and in which races you've ended up on the podium. There's no steadfast rule as to what does and doesn't qualify as part of your *palmarès*, though winning the Tour de France is usually considered a bit more impressive that the round-the-block challenge you won against your best mate as a ten-year-old.

To be considered one of the cycling greats, you'd probably want a clean sweep of all three Grand Tours, all five Monuments and a World Title as well. Only six riders have won the Giro, the Tour and Vuelta. Only three have won all five Monuments. And only one cyclist has won both all three Grand Tours, all five Monuments and the World title as well.

But you know who that is, don't you?

RAINBOW JERSEY
Maillot arc-en-ciel (Fr)/*Maglia Iridata* (It)

It's not actually a rainbow. The five (not seven) colours that make up a cycling rainbow are blue, red, black, yellow and green. If that sequence of colours rings a bell in another context, you'd be right: curl each line up into a circle and you have the five rings of the Olympic logo. The stripes, in other words, follow the Olympic representation of the five continents – although aren't there seven continents, just as there are colours of the rainbow? We should probably move on.

The rainbow jersey was originally awarded at the first World Championships in 1927 and was won by Alfredo Binda. Having won the jersey, the rider is expected to wear it for rest of the year in every equivalent race. So road race winners should wear the jersey in road races, time-trial winners in time-trials and so on (indeed, riders are fined if they don't wear the jersey). The only exception is if you're leading a particular race – so a world champion leading the Tour de France should wear yellow. Once the year as world champion is over, the rider can still wear rainbow stripes on their jersey, such as on their sleeve or collar. But only a current world champion is allowed to wear the rainbow stripes elsewhere; such as the 2015 World Champion Peter Sagan, who as well as the rainbow jersey has sported rainbow-striped shorts, rainbow-striped gloves and rainbow-striped socks, all while riding a bike of blue, red, black, yellow and green. But then he always has been a bit of a colourful character.

One of cycling's enduring myths is the Curse Of The Rainbow Jersey – that having won the Worlds, bad luck is yours for the next twelve months, with a cocktail of poor form and accidents heading in your direction. Yes, there is the tragic case of 1970 world champion Jean-Pierre Monsère, who was killed after being hit by a car during a *kermesse* in Belgium the following spring. And yes, there are any number of riders who have had bad form the following year or suffered from injuries (Tom Simpson breaking his leg skiing after winning in 1965 and Stephen Roche suffering from an ankle injury following his 1987 victory). But all of this is just unfortunate coincidence: tragic coincidence in Monsère's case. Wearing the rainbow stripes didn't stop Binda, Gimondi or Merckx (twice) winning Milan–San Remo. Or Bobet, Merckx, Hinault and LeMond winning the Tour de France. Or Van Looy, Hinault and Merckx winning Paris–Roubaix.

Certainly in 2016 alone, the rainbow jersey hasn't stopped Peter Sagan winning his first Monument or Lizzie Armitstead – the 2015 women's world race champion, – from winning Het Nieuwsblad, the Strade Bianche, Trofeo Alfredo Bina, the Tour of Flanders or the Women's Tour in Britain. Speaking to

Procycling, Armitstead said, 'I think the jersey gives you wings or it does the opposite. It has given me confidence. I feel that I've earned this. You have to beat me, not the the other way round, somehow.'

NATIONAL JERSEY

This follows the same set up as the rainbow jersey: the winner of each country's national road race title gets to the wear the national jersey for the year, with national colours on the collar and shirt sleeves after that. The jerseys differ, but usually have some element of the country's flag in the design. At their best, they can be a design classic – the Italian team in *azzuri* blue are always an arresting sight at the Worlds. At middling, they can look like a flag stuck on the back of a shirt. At worst, you can end up looking like the Colombian women's national team in 2014.

THE YELLOW JERSEY
Maillot Jaune (Fr)

It's a toss up between the *maillot jaune* and the rainbow jersey as to which is the most iconic garment in cycling. Historically, the answer is probably the latter, but the growing dominance of the Tour de France over the last few years – partly due to the likes of Lance Armstrong and Chris Froome shaping their seasons around the race – has meant that the *maillot jaune* has become the most well-known and coveted jersey for a rider to wear.

The *maillot jaune* is a jersey with competing stories about when and where it originated. The usual tale is that it was first worn in 1919, either as the brainchild of organizer Henri Desgrange, or at the request of others involved in the race who wanted a way to pick out the race leader (some cite *directeur sportif* Alphonse Baugé with having the idea). The assumption is that yellow was chosen because it was the colour of Desgrange's newspaper, *l'Auto*. However, other sources suggest that post-war shortages meant that when Desgrange rang up to get the jerseys made at short notice, yellow wool was the only colour available in sufficient quantities.

Eugène Christophe was the first rider to wear the *maillot jaune* in 1919 – assuming one discounts the alternative claim of Philippe Thys, who suggested that he wore one earlier during his victory in 1913. Christophe put on his jersey halfway through the race – without ceremony after stage 10 – and unlike the reverence the jersey receives today, found himself the subject of ridicule, and was heckled by spectators who called him a canary for wearing it.

Today, the only people ridiculed for wearing the *maillot jaune* are that brainless breed of amateur cyclist who think they're Bradley Wiggins rather than a middle-manager from Basingstoke ('Respect the Jersey' as #16 of *The Rules* puts it). For those in the Tour itself, wearing the jersey is a career highlight and there have to be very specific reasons for not putting it on: in 1971, when Eddy Merckx became race leader after Luis Ocaña crashed out, he refused to wear the jersey the following day out of respect. It is Merckx, unsurprisingly, who has more *maillot jaunes* than any other rider (96). Fabian Cancellara is the rider with most *maillot jaunes* without an overall victory (29).

MELLOW JOHNNY

Hilarious US mispronunciation of *maillot jaune* which became appropriated as a nickname for Lance Armstrong. He returned the favour by opening a cycle store in Austin under the same name. Don't, just don't.

THE PINK JERSEY
Maglia Rosa (It)

'The *maglia rosa* is presented to the rider who is the strongest over a three-week period on the most savage and beautiful roads cycling has ever known.' So says *The Rules* and who can argue with that. Unlike the origins of the *maillot jaune* (*see* above), the history of the pink jersey is more widely agreed on: it reflected the colour of the paper of its organizer *La Gazzetta dello Sport* and was first presented in 1931. The first rider to wear the *maglia rosa* was Learco Guerra, winner of that year's opening stage from Milan to Mantua. His nickname was The Human Locomotive.

Once again, it is Eddy Merckx who has worn the race leader's jersey for more stages than any other rider (77). Interestingly, although Fausto Coppi won the Giro five times to Gino Bartali's three, Bartali wore the pink jersey more times (42 times compared to 31).

THE RED JERSEY
Maillot Rojo (Sp)

It makes sense for the leader of the Vuelta to be resplendent in red, what with the colour of the Spanish flag and everything. But the leader's jersey has actually only been red since 2010. Before that it was gold. Before that it was yellow; briefly orange; then yellow before that; orange again; white for a year; and orange once more when the race started in 1935.

ETERNAL SECOND
Eterno Secondo (It)/*Éternel Second* (Fr)

'No one remembers who came in second.' As the American golfer Walter Hagen once famously said. In cycling, however, that's not always the case. Sometimes the runner-up might not have won first prize, but comes away with a different sort of reward.

That is certainly the case with Raymond Poulidor – Pou Pou as he was affectionately known by a generation of adoring French cycling fans. Poulidor is a cyclist with substantial victories on his *palmarès*, having bagged both a Monument (Milan–San Remo in 1961) and a Grand Tour victory (the Vuelta in 1964), but it is what he didn't win – the Tour de France – that earns him his place in cycling history as the 'Eternal Second'.

Poulidor's peak years found himself going head to head with Jacques Anquetil – or shoulder to shoulder anyway, as the duo battled their way up the Puy-de-Dôme in the iconic photo from the 1964 Tour (*See over*). The trouble was that Anquetil was one of the greats; and even when Poulidor got the better of him, as on this particular climb, Anquetil's dominance in the time-trials kept him out in front. Over his career, Poulidor made it on to the podium in Paris eight times, but never once wore the yellow jersey. He achieved a similar feat at the Worlds – finishing on the podium four times but once again never making it onto the top step.

But though Poulidor couldn't beat Anquetil to the *maillot jaune,* he defeated his rival in the battle for public affection. Anquetil could be a hard character to warm to, with his metronomic grind to victory. Poulidor, as the eternal underdog, was easier to root for. When it came to the money-making criteriums after the Tour, it was Poulidor who the public wanted to see: Anquetil might have won the Tour five times, but Poulidor pulled in a higher appearance fee.

What's interesting about Poulidor's record as the eternal second is that he didn't always finish second – out of his eight Tour and four World podiums, he came second four times and third eight. Other riders have finished second more times in the Tour: Joop Zoeltemelk managed it six times; Jan Ullrich managed it five times, or at least he did if we ignore that the results from most of those Tours have since been expunged. Up to that point, Ullrich had found himself handed the eternal second baton, if not the affection that went with Poulidor's reign.

In fact – fittingly – Poulidor wasn't the first to be given the eternal second mantle. The original eternal second was actually an *eterno secondo*: the Italian rider Gaetano Belloni. Just as Poulidor found himself up again Anquetil, so Belloni found his path to the first step of the podium blocked by Constante Girandengo – over his career Belloni finished second to Girandengo a remarkable

25 times. But in the cycling lexicon, the *eterno secondo* will always play, well, second fiddle to Poulidor.

KING OF THE MOUNTAINS
Grand Prix des Montagnes (Fr)/*Gran Premio della Montagne* (It)

The award for the *Grand Prix des Montagnes* was first introduced to the Tour de France in 1933. Prior to that, there had been an unofficial award given by sponsors for the *meilleur grimpeur* ('best climber', *see* Chapter Three). The first winner was the Spanish climber Vincente Trueba, for big climbs over the Ballon d'Alsace and the Galibier. The formula for deciding the winner was the same as today – various levels of points awarded for reaching the summit of mountains of varying difficulty – to calculate who was the best overall climber in the race.

The competition really came into its own in the mid-1970s, with the introduction of the King of the Mountains jersey. In French, this is known as the *maillot à pois rouge* – the 'red peas' jersey; though the polka dot jersey, as it is called in English, has a nicer ring to it. The design is variously ascribed to race organizer Félix Lévitan (as a homage to a 1930s jersey he liked), and to the colours of the jersey's sponsor, Chocolat Poulin: in those two competing stories, you have the Tour's heady mixture of history and commercialization in a nutshell.

Wherever the jersey design originated, like the canary comments Eugène Christophe endured while wearing the original *maillot jaune*, it was not popular to begin with. In *The Great Bike Race,* Geoffrey Nicholson's masterly account of the 1976 Tour, the jersey is described as 'a bit of an embarrassment and will probably be changed.' Instead, it has become one of the sports most recognizable jerseys: in 2010 the Vuelta followed suit and the best climber in that race now wears a blue polka dot jersey. Only the Giro eschews the peas, with the modern winner wearing the *maglia azzura* (blue jersey – historically the best climber wore green). Only two riders have won the competition in all three Grand Tours: Federico Bahamontes in the 1950s and early 1960s, and Luis Herrera in the late 1980s and early 1990s. Bahamontes' six wins in the Tour de France have only been matched by the Belgian Lucian Van Impe and bettered by Richard Virenque.

The inherent problem with the King of the Mountains award is the way it overlaps with the General Classification (GC). Because the overall race is usually won in the mountains, if too many points are allocated to summit finishes, GC riders (such as Chris Froome in 2015) can end up winning the jersey without even trying. But equally, if the points are spread out to counter this, the jersey becomes more of a 'breakaway' award, with lesser riders hoovering up the points of lower mountains earlier in the day. At which point, calling such winners the King of the Mountains feels something of a misnomer, as they are clearly not the best climber in the race.

Below Best of enemies: Anquetil (left) and Poulidor battle up the Puy-de-Dôme at the 1964 Tour

POINTS JERSEY
Maillot Vert (Fr)/Maglia Rosso Passione (It)

The points classification competition was originally run on the fiftieth anniversary of the first Tour de France in 1953. Interestingly, a number of the early Tours were run along more modern points classification lines: between 1905 and 1912, the race was decided not on time, but on points depending on the rider's finishing position. Today, the points competition ostensibly exists to reward the most consistent finisher; occasionally that does happen, as in the case of Peter Sagan – that rare rider who can sprint a bit, climb a bit and get in the breakaways a bit (at the time of writing, Sagan has won the Tour's maillot vert seven times). But usually it is considered more of a sprinter's jersey – assuming the sprinters can make it all the way to the finish and not hop off at the sight of the first mountains, à la Mario Cipollini. Points are awarded for the position of the rider at the finish and also for intermediate sprints during the stage.

That first competition was called the *Grand Prix de Cinquantenaire* and was won by the Swiss rider, Fritz Schaer. Schaer also won the first stage sprint, giving him the race lead, which meant that the first rider to wear the jersey was the Dutch cyclist Wout Wagtmans, who finished second on the stage. The jersey was green, on account of its sponsor, La Belle Jardinière, who made lawn mowers. It has stayed green ever since, with the exception of 1968 when, due to sponsorship reasons, it was red.

The Giro introduced a points classification in its forty-ninth race in 1966, which was won by Gianni Motta. The jersey, introduced in 1969, was mauve until 2009; since then, it has been red – the *Maglia Rosso Passione*. In the Vuelta, the equivalent jersey is green and the competition has been run regularly since the 1950s. However, the Vuelta's point system differs to the other Grand Tours in that it awards equal points for each stage, while in the Tour more points are awarded on flat stages for the sprinters – explaining why the points jersey for the mountain-top heavy 2015 Tour was a battle between climbers such as Valverde, Rodriguez and Chavez.

WHITE JERSEY
Maillot Blanc (Fr)/*Maglia Bianca* (It)

The wearer of the white jersey in the Tour, the Giro and, since 2019, the Vuelta, is the best young rider in the race. The competition started in the Tour in 1975 and in the Giro a year later. The Vuelta's competition didn't begin until 2017, with the first winner of the jersey being Miguel Ángel López. In 2017 and 2018 the jersey was white, with the leader's numbers on a red background (to distinguish from the leader of the combined competition, who also wore a white jersey, but their numbers were on a green background). In 2019, the young rider jersey became straight white to match up with the other Grand Tours.

COMBINED CLASSIFICATION
Clasificacion General Combinada (Sp)/*Maillot du Combiné* (Fr)

The UCI rules about competition jerseys stipulate that only four can be worn in any stage race, in order to keep things simple for the spectator. Before the white jersey shifted to denote the best young rider, the white jersey at the Vuelta was used for the the leader of the combined classification – the rider who is best placed in the general classification, in the mountains and points competitions. It has been awarded since 1970, though with two gaps between 1974 and 1986, and between 1993 and 2002.

Before the start of the best young rider competition, the Tour de France also featured a combined category, with the winner wearing a white jersey. The competition was dropped in 1974, returning in the 1980s with one of the worst jerseys cycling has ever seen – a mish-mash of red polka dots on a white background and splashes of green, yellow and red (the red for the leader in the intermediate sprints).

COMBATIVITÉ (FR)
Combativo (Sp)/*Trofeo Fuga Cervelo* (It)

The English translation of these awards for the most aggressive rider doesn't really do justice to what they're about. We're not talking about a prize for bottle throwing à la Tom Steel or headbutting à la Mark Renshaw. Instead, the award for *combativité* is more about the rider who is, as writer Les Woodland once noted, 'the one who has done the most to liven up the day's stage.' So the rider who has attacked, got in the breakaway, made all the running, if not making it over the finish line first.

The award in the Tour de France is chosen by a panel of esteemed judges on a daily basis (and by TV viewers at the Vuelta). There's no jersey for the winner, but the rider is marked out the next day by his number being white on a red background, rather than the usual black on white. At the end of the Tour, there is an award for the most combative rider throughout the race as a whole.

At the Giro, the equivalent award is the *Trofeo Fuga Cervelo*. Here the winning rider is worked out by the amount of time they have spent in a breakaway at the front of a race: the break has to last for a minimum of five kilometres and have a maximum of ten riders in it. Riders in the group then get a point for every kilometre they stay out front, with the points then totted up to produce a winner.

THE YELLOW RIBBON
Ruban Jaune (Fr)

There is no jersey awarded for winning any of the Monuments or, indeed, any of the Classics. But what there is, is a yellow ribbon – the *ruban jaune*.

First awarded in 1936, this was the brainchild of Henri Desgrange, with his penchant for yellow – one presumes to match the colour of *L'Auto* (though not necessarily; *see* above). The award went to the rider who achieved the fastest average time at any Classic over 200 kilometres in length. Once their record was beaten, the ribbon was passed on to the next rider, and so forth.

In fact, in the 80 years since the prize was first awarded, only twelve riders have had the honour of holding the *ruban jaune*. It was first held by Gustave Danneels of Belgium, who won the 1936 Paris–Tours at an average speed of 41.455 kilometres per hour. Since then, the record has been held by Jules Rossi, Rik Van Steenbergen, Jacques Du Pont, Jo de Roo, Peter Post, Freddy Maertens, Andrei Tchmil, Erik Zabel, Óscar Freire, Marco Marcaten and the current holder at the time of writing, Matteo Trentin. Trentin, like Danneels, also won Paris–Tours, but his 2015 time was somewhat faster at 49.641 kilometres per hour.

Indeed, the majority of the *ruban jaune* holders achieved their time at Paris–Tours (Paris–Roubaix and Paris–Brussels being the other record-breaking races). This is because the *parcours* are pretty flat and usually have a helpful tailwind to boot. When Trentin claimed the *ruban* in 2015, he customised his bike, marking it with a yellow ribbon and details of his time. The had to be changed in 2019 when Philippe Gilbert took the accolade off him: Gilbert won the crazy crosswinds stage 17 of that year's Vuelta (see Echelons), completing the 219.5km at an average speed of 50.63 km/hour.

LANTERNE ROUGE (FR)

'*Lanterne Rouge* is not a position you go for. It comes for you.' So says Wim Vansevenant, winner of the 'accolade' in 2006, 2007 and 2008. It is the name given to the rider who finishes last in the Tour de France – like the *maglia nera* in the Giro in the late 1940s, it can give a rider a certain credence and notoriety. The fact that you've carried on to the end of the race, despite no chance of glory, is a kind of glory in itself.

The term originates from the red lantern placed on the back of the last train carriage, to show that no carriages have got decoupled along the way. Indeed, the last rider is quite often presented with a ceremonial lantern for his troubles at the end of the race. Although the last placed rider of the Tour has always been recorded (in 1903, Arsène Millocheau finished an impressive 64 hours and 47 minutes behind the the winner), the term *lanterne rouge* took some years to be coined. In his excellent book *Lanterne Rouge*, Max Leonard can find no reference to the term before 1919, though the reference, by Henri Desgrange about an 'ex-*lanterne rouge*', suggests the term had been around for a few years before that.

The *lanterne rouge* is a (dis)honour that the race has not always revered as much as the fans. There have been Tours (1939, 1948, 1980) where the last placed rider was thrown out at the end of each stage. The 1980 ruling came about after the battle for last place in the 1979 Tour between Gerhard Schönbacher and Philippe Tesnière: in the final time-trial, the two played a game of chicken in which they tried to go slow enough to finish last, while not going so slow as to be outside the time limit – Schönbacher squeaked in by 30 seconds, Tesnière was 53 seconds too slow and was eliminated.

SIX | Parcours

In Chapter Two, we looked at a race stage from the point of view of the spread of the racing field, from the head of the course at the front to the broom wagon at the back. In this chapter, we'll look at the story of a stage from *départ* to *arrivée*, those important milestones (kilometre-stones?) that the race reels past and takes in on its way to the finish.

LE SIGNATURE (FR)

The school register for cyclists. Before making their way to the start line, each rider has to turn up and sign-on, scrawling their name on the large sheet in the registration area. This has to be done at the Tour at least ten minutes before the start of the race and depending on how the riders feel, they'll either stop and chat to the compère, pose for a few photos with the fans, or just wheel up in dark sunglasses, sign-in and disappear back to the confines of the team bus.

DÉPART FICTIF (FR)

'If I had been going a little bit faster, the spill could have been nasty: it really could have been the end of my Tour before it had begun.' At the 2013 Tour de France, as Chris Froome recalls in his autobiography *The Climb*, he suffered the ignominy of being both the pre-race favourite and also the first person to crash, hitting a concrete barrier on the side of the road.

Fortunately for Froome, the action happened between the *départ fictif* and the *départ reel* (*see* below). This is the short, neutralized section of a Tour stage, where the riders reel out from whatever picturesque starting point the race has chosen and soft pedal for a few kilometres for the locals and TV cameras to get their shots before the race proper starts. When the Tour began in Yorkshire in 2014, the race set off from the centre of Leeds and weaved its way out to Harewood House, where various royals were on hand to cut ribbons and give the race an official ceremonial start. This time Chris Froome saved his falling off until later on in the race.

Froome wasn't the first favourite to find himself on the deck before the start proper. In 1975, Eddy Merckx was still recovering from the effects of being punched by a spectator (*see Tifosi below*) when he found himself tangled up at the start of stage 17: 'Ole, move over!' he yelled at fellow rider Ole Ritter. Ritter, jockeying for position refused to budge, Merckx caught his rear wheel and went down. He broke his maxilla and sinus bone and, as Geoffrey Wheatcroft describes in *Le Tour*, 'his face was wired up so that he could only ingest liquids; he was in acute pain; his doctor told him he must abandon; he rode on.'

DÉPART RÉEL (FR)

Where the proper racing actually begins. Signified by the *commissaire* poking his head through the sunroof of his car and waving his white flag. Often in a less picturesque spot than the *départ fictif*. For the opening stage of the 2014 Tour, it was down a nondescript bit of the A659 on the way to Otley. Prang into a concrete barrier at this point and no-one apart from your teammates is going to hang about for you to catch up.

COMFORT BREAK
Besoin Naturel (Fr)/Call of Nature

Given the length of a one-day race or a tour stage, and also a cyclist's liking for an espresso or two, it's inevitable that at some point the peloton will need to stop for a *besoin naturel* – a call of nature. It's not something you often get to see on the TV as form is for the cameras turn away at such moments: the same is true on the road, as the riders are meant to find a spot where there are no spectators around (sometimes easier said than done).

Quite when the stop happens is usually dictated by the race leader. When he decides to go, that is the cue for all. Making a move to attack at a feeding zone area (*see* below) or when a rider is relieving himself is considered bad form. At the 1957 Giro, there was the case of the 'costly piss': on stage 18, with Gastone Nencini, Charly Gaul and Louison Bobet all vying for the *maglia rosa* (*see* Chapter Five), Bobet and his team stopped for a *besoin naturel.* Gaul pushed on to the fury of Bobet who, when Gaul needed to stop for similar reasons later on, put the hammer down and took his French rival out of the running. Gaul, who the French media nicknamed Monsieur Pi-Pi, could no longer win the race, but was determined that Bobet wouldn't either – on the final crucial mountain stage, he helped Nencini steal the *maglia rosa* by a matter of seconds. Towards the end of stage 16 of the 2017 Giro, history repeated itself when race leader Tom Dumoulin had to take emergency action by the roadside due to stomach troubles: rather than waiting, Ilnur Zakharin took the opportunity to attack, with Bahrain-Merida and Movistar taking turns up to up the pace. Dumoulin lost two minutes to his rivals, but just about managed to cling on to his pink jersey (unlike the contents of his bowels).

Sometimes a rider needs to go on the go: in *Rough Ride* Paul Kimmage describes how during stage 18 of the 1986 Tour, 'I had a fierce urge to piss on the descent of the Croix, but I knew that every second was now precious if I was to beat the time limit, so I pissed off the bike at sixty kilometres an hour.' A rider taken short will engage in a complicated manouevre whereby a teammate steadies the bike, helping them to urinate without stopping. Occasionally, a rider will find good fortune: at the 2014 Tour, FDJ rider Arnaud Démare popped into a spectator's campervan parked up on the side of the road when he needed to use the facilities.

Taking a 'Pou-Pou' is a more complicated procedure. It was easier back in the day when cyclists wore caps rather than helmets. At the 1967 Tour de France, Tom Simpson pulled rank on his *domestique* Colin Lewis, demanding his head gear be handed over: 'I want to have a shit and need to wipe my arse on something.' At the 1986 Tour, Greg LeMond made similar demands of his

teammates after eating a bad peach. 'Taking the small cotton team cap,' Richard Moore wrote in *Slaying The Badger*, 'LeMond shoved it down his shorts, manouevred it into position and filled it until it was over-flowing.' Rejoining the peloton with shit running down his legs, LeMond made it to the finish line, where in his urgency to go and with no toilet in sight, defecated into a box of Bernard Hinault postcards.

FEED ZONE
Zones de Ravitaillement (Fr), Ravitos (Sp), Zona Rifornimento (It)

'Here you go mate, two pork pies and a strawberry yoghurt!'

'Hey, what about my *Cycling Weekly*?'

British cycling fans of a certain vintage will remember the old TV ad for *the* weekly cycling magazine. The ad showed footage of action from the feed zone – that joyous moment in the race when a cyclist will try to grab a *musette* of goodies while cycling one-handed at 40 kilometres an hour (a *musette* being the canvas over-the-shoulder bag containing food and *bidons* or bottles of drink). Getting your grub in the feed zone is no mean feat – especially when there are 100 plus other riders also trying to find their team man at the same time. More often than not, the *musette* ends up on the floor, with a rider then having to go cap in hand to his teammates to see if they've got a spare bit of sandwich. Feed zones were first introduced at the Tour de France in 1919 and were originally more buffet style, with food and drink laid out on tables for the riders to pick up. It is considered bad form to attack in the feed zone – *griller le ravito* – one of those unwritten cycling rules that the peloton takes extremely seriously.

So far there are no reports of a cyclist actually ever having eaten two pork pies and a strawberry yoghurt for their lunch.

INTERMEDIATE SPRINT

During a stage race, each stage will offer up an intermediate sprint. Sometimes called a 'hot spot', the intermediate sprints had their own competition in the Tour de France between 1971 and 1989, with the competition leader wearing a red jersey in the 1980s. These days, the points awarded for the intermediate sprints go towards the green jersey competition, though the points awarded are weighted more towards the stage finishes (and victories). As well as points, there can be time bonuses on offer at the intermediate sprints, as at recent editions of the Giro and Vuelta: at the 2018 Tour, riders could win time bonuses at 'special sprints' on the first eight road stages (for the 2019, these time bonuses were given for eight climbs instead).

NEUTRALIZATION

There can be points during a stage or a race when the riding is neutralized, usually for safety reasons. On stage 3 of the 2015 Tour, the race was neutralized after a 35-man crash in the peloton, including race leader Fabian Cancellara. Tour director Christophe Prudhomme quickly neutralized the race as some teams attempted to capitalize on the crash by putting their foot down. Then he stopped the race completely for ten minutes while Cancellara and the other crash victims made their way back up to the bunch. The argument for the

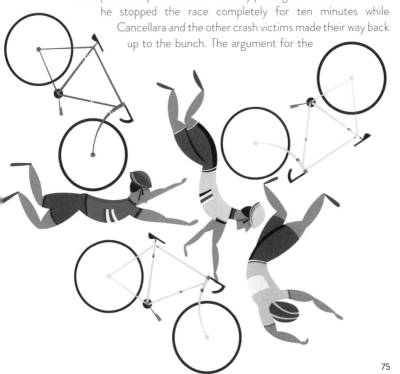

neutralization here was on medical grounds: the Tour's medical staff and ambulances were at full stretch with such a large crash, so to continue the race would have meant going forward without medical support. (Prudhomme's actions were not universally popular, with riders and directeurs sportifs contesting the decision and warning it set an awkward precedent.)

Sometimes bad weather can lead to neutralization. At the 2015 Tour of Oman, one stage was first shortened by a sandstorm and then neutralized after 40-degree plus temperatures led to tyres puncturing on the hot tarmac. At the other end of the weather extreme, snow and freezing temperatures at the 2014 Giro led to the race being neutralized over the Passo dello Stelvio, the race's highest point. Or, at least, that was how some riders and teams interpreted it. Other riders, such as Nairo Quintana, took the commissaire's messages as a warning to be careful: so while some riders were taking it easy down the slopes, Quintana was taking the opportunity to attack. At the end of a confusing day, Quintana had enough time over his rivals to claim the leader's pink jersey.

At the 2019 Tour de France, the pinnacle stage 19 was brought to an early end by a combination of hail, flooding and landslides. Egan Bernal had ridden clear of the other race favourites over to the top of the Col D'Iseran, but with the road ahead to Tignes blocked, organisers had to abandon the stage, and took the time gaps at the top of the Iseran as the end of the stage. It left Bernal taking yellow from race leader Julian Alaphilippe, and a number of riders left to think 'what if'.

END OF FEEDING

The UCI like their rules, one of which is when exactly you're allowed to take refreshments on board. When a race sets off, riders are not allowed to accept food from their team cars for the first 50 kilometres. Should the *musette* in the feed zone not see them through, then any additional food and drink has to be handed over before the '20 kilometres to go' sign. Beyond that, it is considered an illegal feed and riders can face fines and time penalties.

The fines, as UCI fines often are, are pretty minimal – a couple of hundred Euros. But the time penalties can have more serious consequences. On the second stage of the 2015 Tour of Britain, Peter Kennaugh took a gel from the team car with less that fifteen kilometres to go: he got a 20-second penalty, dropping him from seventh to thirty-fourth overall. Two years earlier at the 2013 Tour de France, Kennaugh's team leader Chris Froome found himself 'bonking' on stage 18's crucial second climb of Alpe d'Huez: Froome sent his teammate Richie Porte back to the team car to get him a gel to revitalize him. Without it,

Froome could have lost serious time to his rivals; with the gel, Froome rallied and kept his losses to Nairo Quintana down to just a minute. The 20-second penalty here felt like a price worth paying.

CHAPATTE'S LAW
Loi Chapatte (Fr)

Robert Chapatte was a good, if not great, professional cyclist in the late 1940s and early 1950s. But while his *palmarès* might not be exceptional, he made his name as a commentator in the years following his retirement.

Chapatte is known in particular for his invention of 'Chapatte's Law'. This theorem posits that if the peloton wants to catch a breakaway rider, then at full throttle they can reel them in at a rate of one minute for every ten kilometres of racing left. So if a rider has a lead of over two minutes with 20 kilometres to go, then the chances are that they will stay away until the finish. At some point in the closing stages of a day's racing, the mathematicians in the peloton will therefore be doing the sums and working out exactly when they need to start reeling in an escaped rider.

THE THREE-KILOMETRE RULE

This is the point, towards the end of a race, beyond which if a rider crashes or suffers a 'mechanical' he gets the same time as the group he was with at the moment he stops. The rule has its origins in the Paris–Nice race of 1937, when race leader Roger Lapébie crashed on his way into Marseille's Stade Velodrome for the stage finish. The organizers decided that the group who entered the Velodrome together would be given the same time and Lapébie kept his overall lead. Thirty-five years later, and it was another Paris–Nice finish that helped formalize the rule: this time it was Eddy Merckx who crashed in a sprint-finish in Saint Etienne. He broke a vertebra in the process and lost 42 seconds, which despite protests from rival Luis Ocaña's team, the race organizers decided to cancel out. Merckx didn't go on to win the race (Raymond Poulidor – gasp – taking it overall), but he beat Ocaña despite his injuries – a huge psychological boost for the season ahead.

The rule originally just applied to the last kilometre of a race, but since 2005 has been extended to include the last three kilometres (mountain stages are excluded from this ruling). The rider who crashes still needs to make it over the line to finish the stage. At the 1991 Tour, green jersey leader Djamolidine Abdujaparov hit a barrier at the side of the Champs-Elysées and broke his collarbone. He had to be helped the last few yards over the finish line in order to secure his points jersey.

FLAMME ROUGE (FR)
Red Kite/*L'Ultimo Chilometre* (It)

The *flamme rouge* is there to indicate the 'one kilometre to go' mark in the Tour de France. The red triangle, which these days hangs over the race as part of a giant inflatable arch, was first introduced all the way back in 1906. In terms of the race, it is rarely a deciding moment. If a stage is gearing up for a sprint, the *flamme rouge* is lead-out man territory, with the Cavendishes, Greipels and Kittels all straining to be unleashed over the last few hundred metres. But if you wanted to launch a surprise attack, this might be the moment to go.

THE FINISH
L'Arrivée (Fr)

The UCI, which has rules for most things, has a rule about what constitutes a finish line for a cycling race: a four-centimetre black line in the middle of a 72 centimeter white strip. A rider is over the line when the front of their wheel is on a plane with the start of the black line. That can be tight, and much too quick for the human eye. These days, big races use Lynx cameras, which can break the footage down into 10,000 frames per second. All of those frames can be needed – at stage 7 of the 2014 Tour, Peter Sagan lost out to Matteo Trentin by what was described in one report as the width of a ball bearing; at the 2012 Tour of Turkey, Mark Renshaw beat Matt Goss to a stage win by 0.0003 of a second. Photo finishes were first introduced into the Tour de France in 1954. Before that, judges with clipboards were on hand in what was known as a *mirador*, a tower over the finish line.

The finishing line is also the moment for the stage/race winner to offer up their variation of a victory salute. A well brought-up cyclist will zip up their shirt and emphasize their sponsor's name on the front of their shirt. Some cyclists will take the opportunity to offer up a trademark pose – Alberto Contador, for example, will usually get his *pisteloro* salute out of its holster.

Just be careful not to celebrate too soon. At the 2004 Milan–San Remo, Erik Zabel thought he had the Monument in the bag when he got ahead of Alessandro Petacchi. 'I'm sure I would have won if I'd kept my hands on the bars,' he said afterwards. 'I lifted my hands two metres too soon.' In those two metres, Óscar Freire nipped in to nick the win from Zabel's grasp.

In 2020, Julian Alaphilippe similarly appeared to have got victory in Liège-Bastgone-Liège sewn up. But as he spread his arms wide in celebration, he failed to notice Primoz Roglic haring up his right-hand side and beating him by inches.

SEVEN | Étapes

A Grand Tour – indeed, any type of tour – is made up of a variety of different stages: prologues, queen stages, rest days, time-trials ... all are important parts of a multi-stage road race and make different demands on the riders. For the towns and regions doing the hosting, meanwhile, the demands are more financial...

GRAND DÉPART (FR)
Grande Partenza (It)

Back in the day, the Tour de France would begin as well as end in Paris, the Giro likewise in Milan and the Vuelta in Madrid. But while the Tour and the Vuelta still finish in their respective capital cities, as the Grand Tours have got, well, grander, so have their *départs*. These days, it is not only towns and cities in their native countries that compete for the honour to host the start of a race, but places in neighbouring, or even not so neighbouring countries too.

The first time the Tour de France started abroad was in 1954, when it began in Amsterdam. Since then it has set off from Belgium, Germany, Switzerland, Luxembourg, Spain, Ireland and the UK. The Giro d'Italia started outside Italy for the first time in 1965, in San Marino, and since then the Grande Partenza has been the most adventurous of the three Tours, visiting Monaco, Belgium, the Vatican City, Greece, France, the Netherlands, Northern Ireland, Israel and Hungary. The Vuelta has been a more specifically Spanish affair, with only three starts outside of the country – in Portugal, France and the Netherlands.

The reason for these foreign starts is publicity and financial motives. Beginning a race in a different country increases the profile of the event internationally and is increasingly a feature of top level sport. American Football, for example, regularly plays a handful of league games at Wembley Stadium; in football, the 2020 Spanish Supercopa took place in Saudi Arabia. The only limitation on where such starts can take place is how long it will take to get the riders back to France or Italy for the following stages. In the 1980s, organizer Félix Lévitan even looked into the possibility of the Tour starting on the East Coast of the USA, with the riders being Concorded back to France to continue the race. In May 2016, articles appeared about the possibility of the 2018 Giro beginning in Japan, with the riders being given two days to recover from a climb up Mount Fuji and the flight back to Europe.

The towns and regions competing to host a *Grand Départ* pay handsomely for the privilege: Rotterdam paid £1.96 million (€2.5 million) to Tour organizers ASO for the 2010 start; Utrecht shelled out £3.13 million (€4 million) in 2015; London turned down the opportunity to host the 2017 start, for which the fee was £4 million (about €5 million). And that's without the cost of actually putting the race on. The *Grand Départ* in Yorkshire in 2014 cost £10.6 million; the Utrecht start £11.9 million. However, if you're prepared to stump up the money, the financial benefit to the region is large – calculated to be around ten times the original investment. This was certainly true with Yorkshire in 2014, which saw its economy boosted by £100 million as a result.

As well as the actual start of the race, the hosts of the *Grand Départ* can attempt to get their money's worth. At the 2014 start in Leeds, the city hosted the pre-Tour team presentation at Leeds Arena, with tickets costing cycling fans from £45-85 to watch the riders troop in and out and to listen to music from local nineties Britpoppers Embrace, and Kimberley Walsh and Alistair Griffin sing the *Grand Départ*'s official theme, 'The Road'. Nope, me neither.

PROLOGUE
Prólogo (It/Sp)
A short individual time-trial at the start of a stage race. Prologues were originally introduced into the Grand Tours as a way to wriggle round UCI rules about how many stages a Grand Tour could have: it's not a proper stage, *see*, it's a prologue. As such, the stage is short – under eight kilometres in length and serves as a prelude to the race ahead. It allows the main riders to lay down a marker and reveal an early taste of their form. Because the prologue is short, the time gaps aren't huge: no one has ever won or lost a Grand Tour on the prologue. Well, with the exception of Pedro Delgado at the 1989 Tour: the

defending champion was messing about doing his warm-up round the back and missed his starting time by almost three minutes, putting him out of the running before his feet had even touched the pedals.

The first Tour de France prologue took place in Angers in 1967, with the Giro following suit the next year. The first Tour prologue was just under six kilometres long and was won by the Spaniard José-Maria Errandonea. It was then a regular feature of the Tour for the next 30 years, with a couple of variations: in 1988, it was called a 'preface' and was one kilometre long; in 2005, it was fifteen kilometres long and hence a straight time-trial rather than a prologue. Since then, the prologue has fallen a little out of favour with the Tour organizers. There's an argument as to whether it's good for the race to see the main riders up on the GC so early on, or whether the race is more open in the first week if they start without a prologue. Mark Cavendish was one rider vociferous about starting with a stage proper, to allow a sprinter (such as Cavendish, Mark) a chance of wearing the yellow jersey. The race organisers listened, but Cav failed to take his chance in Corsica in 2013 (stuck behind a crash) or Harrogate in 2014 (crashed himself with the finish line in sight): he finally achieved his goal on the opening stage in 2016, winning the sprint on Utah Beach to claim yellow.

Chris Boardman still holds the record for the fastest Tour prologue, winning in Lille in 1994 at an average speed of 55.152 kilometres per hour (Rohan Dennis went marginally faster in 2015, though that first stage in Utrecht was 13.8 kilometres and so technically not a prologue). Boardman won again in 1997 and 1998, was second in 1996 and may well have won in 1995 had he not crashed out. Given the amount of drugs floating around the peloton during this era, the fact that he took the *maillot jaune* (*see* Chapter Five) three times in this period, and also produced a time that still holds up against the very best today, is a remarkable achievement.

ÉTAPE (FR)
Tappa (It)/*Etapa* (Sp)

'All the world's a stage', as that well-known cycling fan William Shakespeare once had it. If a stage race is as you like it, then a Grand Tour is for you, with its 20-plus components for your delectation over a three-week period. There are different types of stage – flat, mountainous, time-trial, team time-trial (*see* below for the latter two) – with the stages where everyone begins together called *en ligne* or a mass-start stage.

Stages have got shorter – a bit – over the years. The first Tour de France in 1903 was divided up into just six stages, with the shortest (stage 4) at 268 kilometres and the final stage (one of four over 400 kilometres) at 471 kilometres in length. By contrast, the longest day of the 2016 Tour de France is shorter than the 1903 shortest stage (232 kilometres). The longest ever stage of the Tour was 482 kilometres or 300 miles and took place from Les Sables d'Olonne to Bayonne; it was featured in the Tours from 1919 to 1924 (the longest ever stage in the Giro was 430 kilometres from Lucca to Rome in 1914). Since the Second World War, the longest Tour stage has been 359 kilometres from Clermont-Ferrand to Fontainebleu in 1967.

The problem with such long stages was that, firstly, they needed to start in the middle of the night to accommodate such massive distances. Secondly, the riders hated them: 'No one feels like racing,' the journalist Albert Londres wrote in 1924, 'They cross the Vendée, the Gironde and the Landes as though someone they hate is tugging them by the ear.' Thirdly, such long stages increased the incentive for riders to dope or use whatever nefarious means it took just to get them to the *arrivée*.

Finally, there is the question of the race as a spectacle. Sometimes, particularly with the Vuelta, a mountain stage can feel as though it begins with a couple of hundred kilometres of flat nothingness for the first few hours, only bursting into life with a sharp mountain climb at the end that everyone has been waiting for. There's an endurance element in coping with the first few hours, a softening up before the climb, but it can make for quite mundane viewing. In recent years, there has been a vogue for shorter, punchier stages, where the mountains and (hopefully) the action begins earlier in the stage. So in the 2015 Tour de France, the last two mountain stages were just 138 kilometres and 110.5 kilometres respectively, but with plenty of big climbs between them; in the 2018 Tour, organisers trialled a 65 km mountain stage, containing three climbs and a grand prix style grid start. It made little difference to the general classification.

DEMI-ÉTAPE (FR)
Tiers d'Étape (Fr)

One way for Grand Tour organizers to get round UCI rulings about the maximum number of stages – and find a way of pocketing more money by creating more start and finish towns – was the use of split stages. A day could be divided into two stages (*demi-étape*) or even three (*tiers d'étape*). So in the 1937 Tour, riders faced four double-stage and three triple-stage days: day five, for example, saw a 175-kilometre ride from Belfont to Lons-le-Saunier, a 34-kilometre team time-trial from Lons-le-Saunier to Champagnole, and then a final 93-kilometre stage from Champagnole to Geneva.

Such stages meant full coffers for the organizers, but long days for the riders, whose disgruntlement reached boiling point during the 1978 Tour. After stage 11 from Pau to the ski resort of Pla d'Adet, the riders took the ski lift back down to Saint-Lary and then bussed 88 kilometres through traffic jams, not arriving at their hotels until well into the evening. Alarm clocks were then set for 4.30am the following morning in order to begin the first of the day's two stages from Tarbes to Valence d'Agen at 7.30am. After a two-hour break for lunch, there was the day's second stage to contend with – to Toulouse in the afternoon – and then another transfer, this time two hours by train, to reach the start line for the following day's stage.

The race organizers felt that having seen the *parcours* in advance, the riders had accepted them and had some sort of moral obligation to see them through. The knackered riders, however, had different ideas. The morning stage was a go-slow, reaching Valence d'Agen two hours behind schedule. They got off their bikes and walked over the intermediate sprint line, and then did the same at the stage finish, with a young Bernard Hinault leading the way as spectators threw tomatoes at them. Perhaps unsurprisingly, there were no split stages the following year. And although they were reintroduced for the 1980 Tour, their presence in the Grand Tours had fizzled out by the early 1990s. Split stages do still exist, but are generally found in smaller races: on the last day of the 2014 Tour of Britain, there was an individual time-trial in the morning and a circuit stage around the centre of London in the afternoon.

VILLE ÉTAPE (FR)

A town that hosts the start or finish of a Tour stage. To be a *ville étape* involves the local council getting their chequebook out. When Bernard Hinault squared up to the Tour over split stages in 1978, the mayor of Valence d'Agen was particularly affronted as he had paid the equivalent of £10,000 in the hope of putting the small town on the map (which did happen, though not in the way he expected). By the mid 1990s, the equivalent fee had risen to £68,500. Today, estimates vary, though it is known that for stage 2 of the 2014 Tour, York Council paid £500,000 to host the start of the stage and Sheffield £200,000 for the finish. French locales pay less than their international counterparts but still a not inconsiderable amount: the estimated benefits and publicity to a *ville étape* are considered to be double their investment.

INDIVIDUAL TIME-TRIAL
Contre La Montre (or 'CLM') (Fr)/*Tappa a Cronometro* (It)/ The Race of Truth

The individual time-trial (ITT) was first introduced into the Grand Tours at the

Giro d'Italia in 1933. The stage was 62 kilometres long, from Bologna to Ferrera, and was won by the eventual race winner, Alfredo Binda. It was added to the Tour de France the following year, when Antonin Magne won the stage from La Roche-sur-Yon to Nantes.

Riders start in reverse order, with the race leader beginning last. They're pushed off the starting ramp (introduced at the Tour in 1965) at two-minute intervals for a full time-trial (shorter gaps for a prologue). Should you be riding well enough to catch the person in front of you, you're not allowed to advantage yourself by sitting in their slipstream; equally, the overtaken rider is not permitted to hitch a ride in return.

Many riders have their time-trialling skills to thank for their Grand Tour victories – Jacques Anquetil, Miguel Indurain and Bradley Wiggins were all riders who could put huge chunks of time over their rivals against the clock and then hold their own in the mountains. Depending on how generous the Tour organizers are feeling towards the climbers, they will vary the lengths of the time-trials accordingly: the 2015 Tour, for example, had just 13.8 kilometres of individual time-trialling. Sometimes, too, organizers can neutralize the strengths of the time-triallers by having a mountain time-trial: the first one took place in 1939 over the top of the Iséran and there have been other time-trials up both Ventoux (1958, 1987) and Alpe d'Huez (2004).

But the most famous ITT is probably the one that climaxed the 1989 Tour. That year, rather than the regular sprint finish down the Champs-Élysées, the race organizers decided to run the final stage as a time-trial. The result was the closest finish in Tour history, with Greg LeMond overturning a 50-second deficit to snatch the yellow jersey from Laurent Fignon. That said, the climax to the 2020 Tour was also pretty special (see this book's final entry).

TEAM TIME-TRIAL
Contre La Montre Par Équipes (Fr)/ *Cronometre A Squadre* (It)

In 1927, Tour organizer Henri Desgrange had a cunning plan to shake up the race and make it a more exciting spectacle. The problem with the Tour, as far as it had developed, was that all the action took place in the mountains, which meant that the flat stages could be a bit of a non-event. His answer was to have a points competition... no, hang on, that didn't come in for another 25 years. His answer was to turn all of the flat stages into team time-trials (TTT), with each team starting at fifteen-minute intervals. Not knowing how fast their rivals were going, this wheeze would force all the riders to ride at full gas throughout the race, rather than soft-pedalling until the mountains came into sight. Desgrange's plan, it is fair to say, was not a resounding success with the riders or the spectators nor, indeed, did it fulfil his aim of spicing up the race. It meant that the stronger teams dominated the race and thus reduced rather than increased its competitive element. Desgrange tried the plan again the following year, after which he gave up the idea as a lost cause.

But while the TTT got off to a controversial start, this style of racing has developed and grown into a discipline in its own right – and is arguably one of the most memorable sights in modern cycling. There is little to beat watching a team riding in unison; each rider an individual cog in the group's overall performance, and a reminder that while the team leaders might take the glory, modern cycling is very much a team sport. That is reiterated by the rules of a TTT: a team's time is usually taken from the fifth person crossing the line, meaning that a GC contender is only as good as his *domestiques*. At the 2015 Tour de France, Team Sky lost the TTT after the fifth member of the team, Nicholas Roche, lost contact with his teammates: the front four had actually beaten winner BMC's time, but Roche's gapping fifth position cost them the stage.

A good time-trialling team will work as a unit, with everyone taking their turn at the front. In *The Climb*, Chris Froome explains that Team Sky 'have a rule. We look at the speed that we've been given by the man in front of us and try to hold it there for maybe a 30- or 40-second turn, but only on the condition that the speed doesn't drop. If we see the number dip, we pull off straight away.' David Millar in *The Racer* explains how the tactics of the TTT allow you to go flat out at the front in a way that you can't in an individual time-trial: 'The only reason this is possible is because the effort lasts approximately 45 seconds to one minute each time. Then there is recovery time while in the slipstream of your teammates.' Getting the right pace is crucial in TTT success: you want to bury yourself at the front, but not to the point that team members are losing touch at the back. The longer you can keep the whole team together, the more people there are to take turns at the front and the more recovery time you have.

This is one of the reasons why TTT usually take place towards the start of the race (indeed at the Vuelta, the current vogue is for the race to begin with a TTT). The reasoning is to try to ensure a level playing field before riders start dropping out. At the 2015 Tour, the TTT was relatively late in the proceedings as the ninth stage and some teams suffered accordingly: one of the TTT favourites Orica GreenEdge had already lost three members of their team in the first week, with another suffering from damaged ribs in a crash. Essentially a five-man unit against their nine-men rivals, they lost five minutes to the race winners on a 28-kilometre course. Orica GreenEdge, incidentally, hold the record for the fastest Tour TTT with their 2013 stage win clocking in at an average speed of just under 58 kilometres per hour.

LE QUATORZE JUILLET (FR)

The date of 14 July is an important one in French history. This is Bastille Day, the day when the Bastille Prison was stormed to mark the start of the French Revolution of 1789. Today it is commemorated as *La Fête Nationale*, complete with military parades on the Champs-Élysées and celebrations countrywide.

Unless it is allocated as a rest day (something that has only happened six times since the Second World War), *le quatorze juillet* is bang in the middle of the Tour de France, offering French riders an opportunity to restore a bit of national pride by winning the stage, and allowing everyone to forget that the French haven't actually won their own race since Bernard Hinault secured his fifth victory in 1985. Between 1995 and 2005, that appeared to be the order of things, as Laurent Jalabert (twice), Laurent Brochard, Richard Virenque and David Moncoutie all won the Bastille Day stage. However, since then no

French rider won on le quatorze juillet until 2017 when Warren Barguil won, a feat repeated by Thibaut Pinot in 2019. Probably best to whisper it, but the most successful nation in the last fifteen years have been the British, with three stage wins from Froome and Cavendish.

REST DAY
Repos (Fr)
The cycling Sabbath. Such are the demands of a Grand Tour that rest days are required for the peloton to catch their breath. Two are usually allocated in the present-day formulation, though the 2018 Giro had three to accommodate the transfer back from Israel. That hasn't always been the case: early on, there were as many rest days as race ones, with the 1903 Tour spreading its six stages out over nineteen days; then by the 1960s, a single day was a more common occurrence.

One thing the rest day usually isn't, is a day of rest: 'the rest day is more of a reprieve from the mental and physical intensity than a day off,' said Michael Barry in 2012. The cyclists will still cycle, going out for a ride for a few hours to keep their legs ticking over. Less race time means more media work, which for a leader in a modern Tour means sustained questioning over whether or not they are riding clean. 'When I went into the rest day press conference,' Chris Froome recalls in his memoir following his 2013 victory on Ventoux, 'the questions about doping came down like balls of spit from the hills.'

Ironically enough, a lot of the action around doping often takes place on a rest day. Iban Mayo's positive EPO test took place on the second rest day of the 2007 Tour; Alberto Contador failed a test for clenbuterol on the second rest day in 2010 and was banned for two years, despite maintaining his innocence and claiming the reading came from eating contaminated meat. It was also at a 2007 rest day press conference that race leader Michael Rasmussen's line on missing an out-of-competition drugs test started to unravel – with an Italian journalist claiming to have seen him in Italy when he was supposed to be in Mexico – leading to his withdrawal from the race.

But if you're not pissing blood or being grilled by the world's media because of the people who are pissing blood, the rest day can offer you a few moments of normalcy – a brief catch-up with friends and family, a bit of a massage here, a little extra sleep there. However, while relaxing is nice, for the majority of the peloton getting back on the bike is even nicer. In *The Great Bike Race*, Geoffrey Nicholson describes how the riders 'poodle around the paths and through the flower beds like schoolboys on their first bicycles... they really love their bicycles and are unhappy, even ungainly off them.'

TRANSFERS

A long-standing gripe of riders is the use of transfers, where instead of the next stage beginning where the previous one ended, the cyclists are shunted to another location entirely. Sometimes, as when a tour starts in a different country, that is inevitable. But even within the same country, riders can have cause for complaint. During the 2015 Tour of Britain, riders found themselves transported 1050 kilometres over the week-long race, just 400 kilometres less than they had actually raced. 'I've seen a sign for Carlisle every day,' Alex Dowsett complained. 'We've been up and down, up and down Britain, let's start at the top and work down, or vice versa.'

In 1974, the Tour de France came to Britain for the first time – a somewhat curious drag around the Plympton bypass at the behest of Brittany artichoke growers wanting to advertise their wares, and also to publicize the newly opened ferry route between Roscoff and Plymouth. Not that the riders actually went by ferry: they took the plane to Exeter and found themselves at the mercy of British border guards. 'We were treated like illegal immigrants,' said Barry Hoban, who had to kick the door to get the riders out of a locked room. On the way back to France, customs officials delayed the riders by two hours, going through every bag individually, so that the riders did not reach their hotels in France until 10 pm.

In order to have some sort of level playing field, all riders in a race usually have to use the official transport laid on for a transfer, rather than recuperating in a private jet or a luxury coach. In 1991, the Swiss rider Urs Zimmerman eschewed the official plane from Nantes to Pau, partly because he didn't like flying and partly because he wanted a break. So he spent the rest day travelling by car and cycling the last chunk of kilometres to the team's hotel. The Tour organizers removed him from the race: it was only when the rest of the riders refused to start the following stage that he was let back in.

QUEEN STAGE
Étape Reine (Fr)/, Il Tappone (It)/, Etapa Reina (Sp)

The queen stage is the stage within a race that is generally considered to be the hardest and toughest. The origins of the name are a little unclear, though a comparison with chess, where the queen is the strongest piece, is not an unreasonable inference to make.

The queen stage is not an official title, but one bestowed by those following or taking part in the race. It is often not the longest stage in the race and may or may not include the race's highest point, but its combination of climbs and overall brutality will usually make it stand out. That was certainly the case for

stage 11 of the 2015 Vuelta in Andorra, when race organizers invited esteemed climber and local resident Joachim Rodriguez to help design the route. The result was a course that included six major climbs: one category two, four category one, and one *hors categorie*. Won by Mikel Landa, it was a queen stage of queen stages and generally considered one of the toughest Grand Tour days of recent years. Rodriguez himself could only come in fifth, two minutes off the pace.

LES CHAMPS-ÉLYSÉES

There isn't a specific term for the last stage in a Grand Tour race, but the final day has a feel and a rhythm all of its own. It is more processional and ceremonial in tone – more like a criterium or circuit race than a full stage.

Finish in yellow on the final Saturday of a normal Tour, and the race is yours. Sunday is for an obligatory photo of clinking the champagne glass and a finale for the sprinters. For many riders, it is an emotional occasion – confirmation that they have joined the club of those to have completed a Grand Tour. 'The roar from the crowd sent goose pimples through my legs,' remembers Paul Kimmage in *Rough Ride*, 'and though we raced up and down at over 60 kilometres an hour I felt no pain... 132 had finished. I was 131st. I had survived. I was a "Giant of the Road".'

The traditional finish of the Tour has been in Paris, the Vuelta in Madrid and the Giro in Milan. The Giro, however, oscillates between Milan and different locations. With the Tour, the Champs-Élysées has only played host to the end of the race since 1974. For many years, the race wound up at the Parc du Princes track at the bottom of the Bois du Boulogne. When this was demolished in 1967, the close switched to the Piste Municipale at Vincennes. Then in 1974, the move was made to the Champs-Élysées.

Usually, the result has been that the sprinters take the headlines: Mark Cavendish winning four times in a row from 2009 to 2012; Erik Zabel squeaking past Stuart O'Grady to win the green jersey in 2001; Djamolidine Abdoujaparov crashing with the finish line in sight in 1991. Just occasionally, it is the race leaders grabbing the headlines: Greg LeMond and Laurent Fignon in their time-trial duel in 1989; Bernard Hinault and Joop Zoetemelk locking horns in 1979.

As well as functioning as the end of the Tour, in the last couple of years, the Champs-Élysées has also been the setting for something new – La Course, a one-day classic women's race. Run before the men appear, La Course involves a 13-lap traverse of the Champs-Élysées route. The inaugural race in 2014 was won, almost inevitably, by Marianne Vos. Asked about a proper Tour de France for women, Vos has said that she doesn't expect to see it happen while she is still cycling, but at least with La Course, she has been able to experience the magic of racing on cycling's most famous avenue.

EIGHT | The Personnel

Riders wouldn't be riders without the support staff. Welcome to the other inhabitants of the cycling village: those who are there as part of the team; those who are there as part of the race organization; and those who are there dressed up as a devil and jumping up and down on the side of the road.

L'ARDOISIÈRE (FR)

The *ardoisière* is the person with the chalkboard – the term literally means 'slate' – who clings for their dear life to the back of a motorbike, going back and forth between the break and the peloton to tell the riders the time differences. It is a job that had more importance in the past, before race cars had TVs in them and riders had radios with which to chat back to their *directeurs sportifs* (DSs) about what they'd like for their birthday or whatever it is riders and DSs chat about. But it's one that feels like it's an important part of race history and, ironically, looks good on the telly.

For most of the Tour's history, the *ardoisière* has actually been an *ardoisier*. For many years, the job was taken by Joseph Lappatient, ably assisted by Christian Bourgignon doing the actual motorbiking. In 2002, the position was handed over to Michel Bationo. Bationo was from Burkina Faso, where he'd done the same job for a number of years at the country's national tour: he said in a radio interview that he'd love to be the *ardoisier* at the Tour de France, a wish that was heard and then acted upon by officials.

A similar story lies behind the appointment of the current *ardoisière*, Claire Pedrono. By day a financial risk analyst, Pedrono has been an avid cyclist since a young teenager, was a member of the French junior team and a local champion in her native Brittany. When the race organizers came to a nearby event, Pedrono was there with an envelope full of letters and CVs. Pedrono hadn't specifically enquired about being the *ardoisière*, she just wanted to be involved in the Tour. A couple of months later, the race organizers rang up to offer her the role at the Tour of Picardie and from there she hasn't looked back. 'I asked to distribute pens and find myself in the middle of the peloton', as she put it in a 2015 interview.

As with her predecessors, Pedrono's motorbike is still ridden by Christian Bourgignon (day job: restaurateur on Alpe d'Huez) and the two form a skilled double act. Pedrono is not only listening to race radio and updating the riders, she is also watching the peloton closely for any sign of movement or attacks to follow. Bourgignon then has to weave his way through the ever-increasing number of moto-riders buzzing around the race. And if the downhills are hazardous for the riders, they are no easier for the motorbikes, speeding down at over 100 km miles per hour to keep up.

Some of the riders will chat to the *ardoisier* in the hope of gathering a crucial piece of race information. John Wilcockson, who was *ardoisier* when the Worlds

came to the UK in 1970, remembers being summoned over by Eddy Merckx, who wanted to study the board to analyse which riders were in the breakaway. Merckx was satisfied that his teammate Jean-Pierre Monseré was in the break and sat up, concluding that if he tried to reach him, he'd only drag other potential winners with him, reducing Monseré's chances.

Pedrono is one of the very few women directly involved in the race. One would hope that her presence counteracts the anachronistic role of the podium girls (*see* below). But old attitudes die hard, as shown by Christian Prudhomme's reasoning for giving her the job: 'I felt she deserved that honour because of her accomplishments as a cyclist,' he once said, before adding, 'but I have to be honest with you, it doesn't hurt that she has a nice smile.'

BRIGADE ORANGE

The road crew. So called because of the orange overalls they wear, the *brigade orange* are the team who build the start, the finish and the village. Then they work into the night to take it all down and set it up elsewhere for the following day's stage. The *brigade orange* are also responsible for the state of the road itself – tarmacking a pothole here, or ramping a speed bump there.

TIFOSI (IT)

Cycling is one of the great spectator sports in terms of the display on offer. What's more, it's free. Unlike most elite sporting events, where you can find yourself forking out hundreds of pounds for a ticket, the only thing you have to do to watch the Tour or Giro whizz by, is get yourself to the roadside (and by the roadside very early if you want a prime spot). Each year, it is estimated that 12 million fans line the roads of France to watch the Tour: when the race came to Yorkshire for the *Grand Départ* in 2014, an estimated 2 million turned out to watch it.

Some fans are more hardcore than others. 'For the past 13 years,' William Fotheringham recalled in 2002 *Put Me Back On My Bike,* 'on every single stage I have driven – perhaps 200 – I have seen the same Belgian camper van pulled up on verges from Nice to Nantes, driven by a 75-year-old named Lucien Blio from a village in Flanders... Blio began following the Tour in 1974 and is as much part of the race's furniture as Lance Armstrong. It is admirable,' he concludes, 'but not normal.'

Fans from Flanders have a reputation for being particularly passionate and knowledgeable. Talking about Paris–Roubaix in Ian McGregor's *To Hell On A*

Bike, journalist Daniel Friebe said, 'The atmosphere isn't as good as the Tour of Flanders. It's more of a Tour de France atmosphere. People, especially along the route, just go to applaud or, "it's great, we're going to watch Paris–Roubaix," whereas at the Tour of Flanders they're really into it.' That tribal element amongst Flemish fans has been a long-standing part of cycling there: to the point of never fully warming to Eddy Merckx for being from the wrong part of Belgium.

In Italy, the *tifosi* have always been central to the success of the sport. These are fans who will offer vociferous support to the riders they like and make life hard for those they don't. In the late 1940s, as two Italian greats – Coppi and Bartali – did battle, Italy took sides as well: you were either *Coppiani* or *Bartaliani.* Coppi's fans were usually from the north of Italy, younger, more urban; Bartali's support was strongest in Tuscany, in the centre and south of Italy, and had a stronger religious bent. One particular Coppi fan was Enrico Locatelli, who introduced Coppi to his wife Guila Occhini. Coppi and Occhini began an affair: when the press found out, she was dubbed the 'White Lady' and Occhini arrested for adultery. The affair was a national scandal and Coppi's reputation never recovered.

In France, the cycling fans have a longstanding indifference to winners. It stretches back to preferring 'Pou-Pou' to Jacques Anquetil and is a line that encompasses Eddy Merckx, Miguel Indurain, Lance Armstrong and Chris Froome. The enmity towards the last two reflects a combination of rooting for the underdog, a dislike of the way teams like US Postal and Team Sky go about their business, and suspicions about drugs (unfounded in Froome's case). Froome is paying the price for the behaviour of his predecessors and being booed and spat at seems to be part of his lot. It's a peculiarity of his relationship with the Tour: at the Vuelta, there are no such comparable scenes.

It probably doesn't make Froome feel much better, but it's the sort of behavior that French fans save for only the most successful riders. And at least he hasn't suffered the sort of altercation that Eddy Merckx experienced during the 1975 Tour. On the climb up the Puy de Dôme, Merckx was punched in the stomach by Nello Breton. Breton was arrested, charged and ordered to pay Merckx a symbolic one franc in damages. But it was Merckx who really paid: the bruising and inflammation did for him, and though he struggled on to Paris, the pain and Bernard Thévenet got the better of him.

THE DEVIL
El Diablo (Sp)
Arguably the most famous fan of the last couple of decades, Dieter 'Didi'

Senft is best known to cycling aficionados around the world as *El Diablo* or the Devil. Senft is a longstanding cycling fan and amateur cyclist from former East Germany. In 1993, he dressed up in his devil costume for the first time – this was in honour of rider Claudio Chiappucci, whose nickname was *El Diablo* and of whom Senft was a huge fan. Although Chiappucci retired at the end of the 1990s, Senft has remained a regular sight at both the Giro and the Tour de France.

Senft likes to find a relatively unpopulated spot and gets there early to paint his pitchforks on the road, to warn the cyclists who they are approaching (in one interview he claimed to use 50 litres of white paint per Tour). Then, when the riders approach, he brandishes the relevant pitchfork (he has 20 in his collection) and runs alongside them as they cycle past. Senft claims to be respectful of the riders, running behind them and trying not to get in their way, though he describes how many cyclists steer to the opposite side of the road. But mostly, he is a popular figure on the road, an altercation with the Italian police excepted: they took a dim view of Senft painting his pitchforks all over a piece of road that had been newly tarmacked especially for the Giro.

When Senft isn't chasing Grand Tour riders, he is back home in Germany making bizarre bicycles. In 2008, he entered the Guinness Book of World Records for making the world's largest mobile guitar bicycle, at four metres tall and fourteen metres long. Though quite how much competition he had from other mobile guitar bicycles out there is unclear.

MECANO

'That's the difference between a mechanic's job and *soigneur*'s job. A mechanic's job, if you fuck it up, it can actually cost the race. A *soigneur* can't really fuck up. I mean, how do you fuck up a massage?' Kris Withington in *Bike Mechanic* succinctly describes the lot of a *mecano*. A mechanic for Garmin, Withington was there the day David Millar's chance of winning a stage at the 2008 Giro disappeared when, as part of a five-man break, his chain snapped with one kilometre to go: 'in one furious moment, I was off the bike, standing in the road and, in a red mist, hurling the bike powerfully over the crowd barriers,' he recalled in *Racing Through The Dark*. 'That was a bad day,' Withington agreed, 'worse was we didn't know what the problem was.' The fault turned out to be a bad run of Shimano chains that everyone thought someone else had checked. But while Millar's bike got it in the neck, his mechanic didn't: 'We finished work and were at the hotel, and David was sitting at the bar and said to me: "Hey Kris, come on" – and we had four beers.'

A mechanic's lot is a thankless one, though the riders generally seem to understand this and, like David Millar, are appreciative of their efforts. Their home is 'the truck', a sort of mobile workshop where they clean, fix up and make good bikes between stages. During a race itself, they are as onhand as they are allowed to be: at large races, a neutral service car is always second place in the convoy of cars behind that of the race director; the team cars sit further back, ready to be called forward when needed by race radio.

This is all a long way from the early history of the Tour de France, where riders were expected to do all their own repairs and received punishment if they accepted help in fixing their bicycles. At the 1913 Tour, future Tour winner Eugène Christophe was hit by a car on the Col du Tourmalet, which broke the fork on his bicycle. He carried his bike ten kilometres down to Ste-Marie de Campan, where he set about fixing it single-handedly in a blacksmith's forge. At one point, a young boy pumped the bellows for him while he worked, for which an eagle-eyed official docked him ten minutes.

For any mechanic, the biggest day of the year is Paris–Roubaix. As Guy Andrews writes in *Bike Mechanic*, 'it is the race with the most problems, the most punctures, the most crashes and the most stress. Yet ask any mechanic to name their favourite race to work on and Paris–Roubaix will be it.'

SOIGNEUR (FR)
Swanny

Soigneur is a French term that is derived from the word *soigner,* meaning 'to care'. In cycling terms, it is a phrase that encompasses a number of different tasks, whether that is preparing the food, schlepping suitcases from hotel to hotel and running errands, to providing the after-race massage, a shoulder to cry on and an ear to listen to a rider's troubles. Geoffrey Wheatcroft suggests in *Le Tour* that 'riders often have a relationship with their *soigneur* at least as close and trusting as any golfer with his caddy.'

A *soigneur*, therefore, gets to know a rider extremely well: Guillaume Michiels, Eddy Merckx's *soigneur*, estimated that during 1970, he spent 340 days on the road doing the bidding of the Cannibal. There are many legendary *soigneur* figures throughout cycling history – Raymond Le Bert, for example, was intrinsic to Louison Bobet's success in the mid-1950s. The most famous *soigneur* of them all is probably Giuseppi 'Biago' Cavanna, who looked after Fausto Coppi, among others. Cavanna was blind, losing his sight in his mid-forties after dust got into his eyes, but his rider considered that he had *il tatto*, the 'healing touch' in his hands: 'my hands can see better than any human eye', Cavanna claimed, saying that 'massaging [Coppi's] legs was like playing a guitar.' Among his nicknames were The Miracle Maker and The Muscle Wizard, but Cavanna's gifts went well beyond his massage skills: he was also a trainer, a tactician and an all-round cycling guru whose riders were as devoted to him as he was to them.

More recently, the role of the *soigneur* has become a little less credited thanks to their role in a string of doping allegations. Willy Voets was the *soigneur* of the Festina team in 1998, whose car was stopped by the French police and found to have a whole stash of EPO and assorted other drugs hidden away. Emma O'Reilly, meanwhile, was the *soigneur* to Lance Armstrong's US Postal Team – one of a very small number female *soigneurs*. She described her role in a 2014 interview as being 'like a big sister. I was feeding them, massaging them, cleaning them up after they had finished, making sure they had clean clothes, so it was quite a caring relationship.' The family feud that followed is well documented elsewhere, not least in O'Reilly's own book *The Race To Truth* – and needn't trouble the lawyers here.

CARAVANE PUBLICITAIRE

'There was a distant volley of silly musical horns and as a sort of Mexican cheer spread slowly up the road [Mrs Belgium] rushed to the tarmac, clapping her hands, slapping her haunches and constructing facial expressions consistent with a triple jumper psyching himself up at the start of his final run up: the free crap is coming.' (*French Revolutions*, Tim Moore)

One of the most depressing statistics relating to the Tour is from a survey on the official Tour de France website stating that 47 per cent of the people who turn out to watch the Tour are there, first and foremost, to see the publicity *caravane*. Forty-seven per cent. Good grief. And people wonder why cycling fans prefer the Giro or the Classics (not that these are immune either – the

Giro has its own *caravana*, though nothing on the scale of the Tour's version).

The *caravane* was a scheme first dreamed up by Tour organizer Henri Desgrange back in 1930. To break up the dominance of the trade-sponsored teams in the race, Desgrange reformulated the Tour into national teams, with riders all having to use the same bike provided by the Tour organization. To fund this, he formalized what had already been happening – capitalizing on the different firms that followed the Tour around advertising their wares, he now made them pay for the privilege of being part of the *caravane*, a rolling flotilla of vehicles preceding the race itself.

Below 'The free crap is coming': the
Tour de France *caravane publicitaire*
1950s style

The modern *caravane* is huge. Depending which report you read, it is between twelve and 25 kilometres in length, snaking its way along the Tour route, throwing out freebies to the waiting fans. Today the *caravane* features just under 200 vehicles and takes a good 45 minutes to pass by. Over the course of the Tour, an estimated sixteen million items are handed out. At the 2014 Tour, Yorkshire Tea handed out five million tea bags packed into limited-edition Yorkshire Thé boxes; sausage manufacturer Cochonou flung out just under half a million taster packs, estimated by Inrng.com as being one pack for every seven metres of the race route. It's not cheap as advertising campaigns go – sweet manufacturer Haribo reckons that the cost of the giveaways (1.5 million bags of sweets in their case), the €250,000 fee paid to the organizers, the staff and the vehicles adds up to a bill of €1 million for the duration of the race. But it works: firms involved in the 2014 *caravane*, such as Cochonou, reported a 20 per cent increase in sales.

For the real cycling fan, it might all seem a bit gaudy, but as Tim Moore says in *French Revolutions*, it's a little difficult to get on too high a horse about these things when you're watching a race originally set up to advertise a newspaper. So while it might seem like commercialization at its worst – and yes, some people even leave the roadside with their freebies before the cyclists even show up – the *caravane* is part and parcel of the modern Tour spectacle.

DIRECTEUR SPORTIF (FR)

'I rode for Jean de Gribaldy for the best part of ten years and he was as intimidating the last time I saw him as he had been the first day we met... De Gribaldy believed in hard racing, lots of training and eating little. He kept his riders hungry, in a very real sense.' Sean Kelly, in the appropriately titled, *Hunger*.

At the heart of every great cycling team is its *directeur sportif* (DS) – the sporting director in charge of training, of team selection for each race, and for team tactics within the race itself. It is a role that has often been filled by strong individuals – Jean de Gribaldy keeping Sean Kelly in his place, Cyrille Guimard getting the best out of Bernard Hinault, Laurent Fignon and Lucien Van Impe, for example. At its best, the relationship between rider and DS empowers them both: the latter mentoring the former to greatness by knowing how to get the maximum out of them. That was certainly the case with Guimard and Hinault at the infamous Liège–Bastogne–Liège in 1980: while others were quitting left right and centre, Guimard had warm dry clothes, hot tea and a fresh bike with low gears waiting for his rider; he even told Hinault to take his racing cape off, forcing the Badger to rider harder to keep warm.

At its worst, the relationship between rider and DS can destabilize the team. Laurent Fignon said of the deteriorating relationship between Hinault and Guimard in 1982 that 'we could feel it, like gangrene, slowly letting its toxins into the team day by day.'

These days, the role of the DS has increased during the race itself thanks to the ability to be in constant communication with the riders. With a TV monitor to watch the race, the DS can issue instructions and change tactics in a way they couldn't 30 years ago. The fact that a number of DS are former riders themselves is no coincidence: their reading of the race is increasingly part of the job.

COMMISSAIRE (FR)

The cycling equivalent of a referee in football or an umpire in cricket, the *commissaires* are the people mandated with maintaining the (many, many UCI) rules of the race, and reaching all those decisions about who pushed who in the sprint, who won the photo finish, and how lenient to be in deciding the time limit and which riders to eliminate from the race.

Lenient probably isn't the right word – stiff is probably a better description. A *commissaire*'s lot is to get it in the neck from the riders and the media for reinforcing a string of cycling rules, rather than using a bit of common sense when interpreting them. On stage 10 of the 2015 Giro, GC contender Richie Porte punctured as the race entered the final kilometres; at which point Simon Clarke, who was not in contention for the overall, offered Porte his wheel, so he wouldn't lose too much time. Porte raced to catch up and managed to keep his losses down and GC hopes alive. Clarke, meanwhile, was lauded for helping out a rider from a rival team...

...but then, once the *commissaires* got their rulebook out, Porte was handed a two-minute penalty for 'non-regulation assistance to a rider of another team.' As Porte's boss Dave Brailsford said afterwards, 'It just goes to show you either live by the letter of the law or the spirit of the law. Most people would accept that was one of the most interesting, instinctive bits of fair play we've seen in sport for a long time, particularly our sport, which has been a bit blighted by issues of unfair play.'

That's just one of many examples of such rulings from the *commissaires*. Two years earlier at the Tour de France, Cannondale rider Ted King was eliminated from the race for finishing outside the team time-trial time limit by just seconds. King was recovering from the effects of a heavy crash on the Tour's opening stage, which occurred when the *commissaires* created chaos by moving the start line forwards and then back because of a bus stuck at the finish line. Rules, though, were rules and out he went.

During a stage, the *commissaires* split up to try to keep an eye on everyone from the front to the back of the race. Some riders feel they can be singled out for special treatment. 'The race jury had seemingly deployed one *commissaire* solely to watch me,' Mark Cavendish complained in *At Speed* about the 2011 Tour, with the individual in question 'a constant, irritating presence at my side.' Every time Cavendish stopped for a toilet break, the *commissaire* held up the convoy of cars to wait, rather than allowing Cavendish the usual procedure of slipstreaming his way back up through the cars to rejoin the race.

No doubt, being a *commissaire* is a difficult job and like a football referee, you're going to get criticism whatever ruling you come to. But as Dave Brailsford noted, one does wish they would sometimes up the spirit rather than the word of the law.

PODIUM GIRLS
Hostesses du Tour (Fr)

One of those old-fashioned elements of cycling whose time, surely, is numbered. Yet like ring girls in boxing, the presence of the *hostesses du Tour* is a standard element of most major cycling events. Traditionally the women at the day's presentation would be local – the only rules being that they were under 30 years old and roughly the same height. But today, it is an attractive gig, and massively over-subscribed by potential models: at the Tour, the sponsors of the four jerseys choose the hostesses for their particular competition.

For a *hostess*, the actual day on Tour is a long one, with the presentation ceremony only a small part of it: they have to be there early in the morning to entertain their sponsor's guests at the *village* and continue on from there. Endurance and personality are as important for a successful *hostess* as how they look. One former *hostess*, Laura Antoine, recalls being asked if she could still smile when she was tired – a question that she discovered was all too pertinent for the job ahead.

The combination of attractive women, young athletes and a rule that fraternization is forbidden is always going to be a recipe for trouble. On the podium itself, it can lead to awkwardness, missed lunges and uncertainty as to how many kisses is the right number: 'I never know what to do at that point, and to tell you the truth a lot of girls don't know what to do with me either', David Zabriskie told the *New York Times* in 2010. Equally awkward in a different way was Peter Sagan's squeezing of Maya Leye's bottom during the award ceremony for the 2013 Tour of Flanders. Sagan later apologized, though the

photo of him grabbing Leye's behind while Leye was kissing race winner Fabian Cancellera sadly seemed to sum up the attitude of many in the modern peloton.

Off the podium, there are plenty of stories of seduction involving any number of riders you care to mention. Jens Voigt claims he can name at least ten former colleagues who got married to a podium girl. Perhaps the most famous rider-*hostess* romance is that between George Hincapie and Melanie Simmoneau in 2003: 'I pretty much ended up chasing her throughout the whole Tour,' Hincapie later recalled, 'I finally got her number and she said, "I'm totally not allowed to talk to you."' When the couple were caught texting each other, Simmoneau was given an ultimatum by the organizers to finish it or quit the podium. She chose the latter, and the pair went on to get married and have two children.

NINE | The Roadbook

The roadbook is that magic cycling document that tells the team the route of the race, mapping out the kilometres and giving them much-needed information about the road ahead. However, the route isn't just about the gradient or that final bend on the way to the finish; it can be as much as about the weather, the terrain, or the other unexpected obstacles that a victorious rider needs to overcome...

THE STRADE BIANCHE
La Strade Bianche (It)

If Belgium and the north of France has its *pavé*, then the hills of Tuscany have what the locals call their *sterrati*. These picturesque, white gravel dirt roads form the backbone of the Strade Bianche (literally 'white roads'), the early spring semi-classic that has quickly cemented itself into the cycling calendar since its launch in 2007. As with Paris–Roubaix, the one-day race features a litany of these dirt road sectors – ten sections of around 50 kilometres in total – designed to break up the rhythm of the race.

Racing on gravel has some similarities to riding on *pavé* in that when its dry, it is incredibly dusty: anyone riding these roads can end up looking like they've been in a flour fight by the end of the race. Equally, when the roads are wet, they can be lethal – a slip-sliding lack of grip when going downhill. And as with the northern Classics, positioning on the Strade Bianche is everything: if you're not at the front, you can't see what's coming, can't choose your line, can't get out of the way if someone falls; you can find yourself blocked in, rather than being able to attack. But these roads are more compacted and faster to ride on than cobbles – bone-shaking and puncture-friendly, yes, but not as much of an endurance test. And the fact that the weather tends to be better doesn't hurt either.

There's something quite timeless about racing on these roads. Indeed, the Strade Bianche started on the back of L'Eroica, a retro sportive that was first run in 1997. In this race, competitors have to use bikes made before 1987 and clothing has to be similarly old-fashioned – wool jerseys and casquettes. Certainly, both the sportive and the pro-race make full use of the Tuscan countryside, with the Strade Bianche finishing in the centre of Siena. The most successful rider has been Fabian Cancellara, who has won the race three times since its inception and has been rewarded for his efforts with one of the sectors being named after him for future editions of the race.

SAND

At the 2015 Vuelta, the race organizers had a plan for a dramatic and visually stunning opening stage – a team time-trial along the coast of the Costa del Sol from Puerto Banus to Marbella. But while the views were eye-catching, the road surface was somewhat less impressive. The route included a rickety ride along the beach on plastic boards and a stretch of coastal track under an inch of hot Spanish sand. It didn't take long for the riders to start complaining and posting their concerns on social media: sand is skiddy to ride on, which is the last thing you need when you're bombing along at close to 60 kilometres per hour for a flat-out team time-trial. In the end, the stand-off saw a compromise – the team time-trial would go ahead but would be neutralized in terms of individual general classification. It meant that several teams played it safe and took it easy on the run-in.

Sand can be a problem for cyclists, not just on the ground but also in the air. With the early cycling season spending time in the Middle East, there can be problems traversing the desert in events such as the Tours of Oman and Dubai. Indeed, one stage of the 2015 Tour of Oman was first shortened and then neutralized after the start of the race was hit by a sandstorm, swirled up by 70-kilometre-per-hour winds.

But sand can also be a saviour in certain situations. In his autobiography *The Climb,* Chris Froome describes riding for the Kenyan team in the 2006 Tour of Egypt. One of his teammates, Michael Muthai ended up off the back of the race. Missed by the broom wagon and with Froome's team car elsewhere (off sight-seeing at the pyramids), Muthai found himself stuck in the desert. To try and keep himself cool in the desert heat, Muthai dug himself into the sand, until someone came past to pick him up (a driver from a Polish team eventually found him, having had to drive back to collect some chargers).

HEAT

At the other end of the spectrum from the snow and ice of the spring Classics and the Giro, are the difficulties faced by riders when the mercury starts to soar. At the Tour de France and the Tour of Oman in 2015, riders had to cope with temperatures of nudging 40 degrees. And that's not as hot as it gets – as the tarmac soaks up the sun it heats up still further, the roadside radiating temperatures up of 50, 60 degrees, even higher.

These sort of weather conditions bring with them a whole variety of problems. Firstly, there is the effect on the road surface: on the descent of the Cole de Manse at the 2003 Tour de France, Lance Armstrong described the corners as 'melting' and the asphalt 'bubbling'. Joseba Beloki, second in the overall rankings and taking risks on the descent, hit a pitch of melted tarmac, skidded and went over. He broke his right femur, elbow and wrist, finishing his Tour and (arguably) his career. Armstrong, meanwhile, took evasive action across a field to rejoin the race.

Secondly, there is the effect on the bike tyres. During the sandstorm-affected stage of the 2015 Tour of Oman, the riders took shelter under a bridge to discuss their safety concerns about riding in such heat: 'The steepness of the downhill and the temperatures were too much, the tires and wheels couldn't release the heat enough,' explained Boonen. 'It's life-threatening when you're going 90 kilometres an hour and the tyre explodes.' Race organizer Eddy Merckx was not entirely sympathetic with the complaints – 'Riders' security? Well what about Paris–Roubaix when it rains?' – but the stage was eventually cancelled.

Thirdly, and most importantly, there is the effect of the heat on the riders themselves. It is hot work out there in the baking sunshine and while the riders create some breeze when bombing along which cools them down, as they start going uphill, the loss of energy, the risk of dehydration and of heat exhaustion really begins to soar. At the 2015 Tour, Thibaut Pinot was one rider who lost large chunks of time because of the temperatures: 'I've come to realize the last few days that as soon as it gets hot, I quickly lose energy. The heat is a mountain.' Cannondale rider Nathan Haas described the heat as 'very attritious [sic] It's something you can't describe, the feeling that when the heat gets so deep within you that it feels like it's in your bones. It can happen before you realize and it can take a long time to cool down.'

Keeping yourself hydrated in such temperatures is crucial. Pity the poor *domestique* going back to the team car to fetch more water bottles; riders can easily drink 25-30 *bidons* on a hot stage. According to Lotto-Soudal team doctor Jan Mathieu, a rider loses ten per cent of their energy for every one per cent of their body weight that they sweat out: 'A sportsman who weighs 70 kilograms and loses almost three litres of water during his effort loses 40 per cent of his strength,' he told AsiaOne in 2015. 'The rule is to drink two bottles per hour, that's one litre.' Downing such volumes of liquid wasn't always an option in years gone by. At the Tour, riders were permitted two *bidons* on their bike at the start, another couple in their *musette*, and that was it, beyond what they could grab from fans on the roadside. Extra bottles from the team weren't allowed, because of suspicions about riders getting a free ride.

In the grand scheme of things, that was probably the wrong priority. In 1958, Fausto Coppi accepted an invitation to race in Colombia, becoming seriously unstuck on the *El Colombiano* Classic. The race went from Medellín to La Pintada and back again, taking in the notorious Alto des Minas. With temperatures of 40 degrees in the shade and a severe gradient, the local riders took full advantage of the conditions. First Coppi's *domestique* Ettore Milano abandoned, suffering from the sunstroke. Then it was Coppi's turn to be hit by the heat, as described by one spectator in Matt Rendell's *Kings of the Mountains:* 'His face was pale and bloodless. He was pedalling unbelievably slowly. As he drew closer, he wobbled violently, then right at my feet – he collapsed. I looked away and when I looked back, I saw his face was green and his lips yellow. His eyes were rolling, mostly white. He was soon surrounded by medics and *soigneurs* trying to bring him round.'

Nine years later, tragedy befell the British rider Tom Simpson on the slopes of Mount Ventoux during the 1967 Tour. As the race made its way towards the summit, Simpson collapsed and died from a deadly cocktail of amphetamines, dehydration and heat exhaustion. His death was the culmination of a number of similar incidents in previous Tours: Jean Malléjac, also on a baking hot day on Ventoux in 1955, was unconscious by the roadside for fifteen minutes. According to William Fotheringham's *Put Me Back on My Bike*, 'cyclists of the time seemed to have been half-aware of the dangers of extreme heat: there was an unwritten convention that they did not use amphetamines or other stimulants in such conditions.' Simpson did, and paid the ultimate price.

As temperatures continue to rise due the effects of climate change, questions over rider safety and hot weather are bound to get increasingly, well, heated. At the 2018 Tour Down Under, organisers dealt with high temperatures by reducing one stage by 26 km and starting another an hour earlier to avoid the hottest part of the day. Some months later, at the 2018 Volta a Portugal, organisers were less flexible even though temperatures on one stage reached 47.5 degrees celcius (117 Farenheit). Instead, local firefighters lined the route and sprayed the peloton with water as they passed through each district.

LEVEL CROSSINGS

The usual rule of the road when one approaches a level crossing is quite simple: if the lights start flashing and the barriers come down, it's time to put on the brakes and sit up, until the train has passed. In a cycling race, however, common sense has a habit of going completely out of the window.

At the 2015 Paris–Roubaix, the race route crossed a train track with 85 kilometres to go. When the barriers started to go down as the peloton approached, the majority of the riders decided the best response was to speed up rather than slow down, weaving their way across the track. On that occasion, there were a handful of seconds between the riders crossing the track and the train thundering past. However the same month, at the U-23 Tour of Flanders, the time between rider and train was even smaller – with the last rider squeezing across to the sound of the engine's horn.

Not that this is a new phenomenon. On YouTube, there is black and white footage from the 1937 Paris–Nice race that looks like an episode of the Keystone Cops, as riders climb over the gates to get out of the way of a steam train. Go further back to Paris–Roubaix in 1919, and winner Henri Pélissier got round a train that had stopped at the level crossing by carrying his bike aboard, opening a door on the other side, then clambering down and carrying on. Earlier still, at the 1914 Giro d'Italia, the peloton pulled up at a level crossing 15 kilometres into a mammoth 430-kilometre stage from Lucca to Rome. All the peloton, that is, except Lauro Bordin who used the cover of darkness to slip across unnoticed. He managed to stay away for fourteen hours and 350 kilometres before finally being reeled in.

Bordin certainly wasn't the only rider to try to use a level crossing to his advantage. At the 1907 Giro di Lombardia, Giovanni Gerbi, depending on which account you read, either used a couple of riders to slow up the peloton while he gave them the slip, or had a roadside associate throw a bike at his pursuers to let Gerbi get ahead. Either way, in a pre-planned move, the

Above Train trouble at the
1949 Tour de France

remaining riders came to a closed level crossing, which Gerbi had successfully cleared and which his supporters kept shut behind him. Gerbi won the race by 40 minutes, before being stripped of his title. When Robert Millar (now Philippa York) lost the race lead of the 1985 Vuelta in the race's pinnacle stage, there was the suspicious story of the The Train That Never Came. Isolated and in need of his teammates, two of Millar's *domestiques* (see Chapter Three) attempted to catch him up, only to find themselves stuck at a level crossing. They waited and waited, but no train ever arrived – by the time it opened again, catching Millar was impossible and a cycling conspiracy tale was born.

Giovanni Gerbi isn't the only rider to have been disqualified for level-crossing shenanigans. The UCI rules about level crossings are that anyone who crosses after the barriers are down is at risk of disqualification. While that didn't happen at the 2015 Paris–Roubaix race because of the sheer number of riders who tried it, nine years earlier, the riders who finished second, third and fourth were all disqualified for ignoring the barriers with 15 kilometres to go.

ANIMALS

It's the second stage of the 2013 Tour and the riders are heading into the outskirts of Ajaccio for the stage finish. With four kilometres to go, a small group of half a dozen riders had about ten seconds lead on the peloton, which were chasing hard to catch them up. Then suddenly, in the middle of that gap, a little white dog – a West Highland Terrier – runs into the middle of the road. His owner runs into the road to retrieve him; then, seeing the speeding peloton about turns and runs the heck out of the way. The Highland Terrier, meanwhile, takes his own evasive action and sprints for the opposite side of the road. Carnage, this time, averted.

Animals, and dogs especially, have something of a track record when it comes to cycling races. The first such incident took place right back in the first Tour de France, when on the fourth stage from Toulouse to Bordeaux, a dog took out fifteen riders. In the 1940 Giro, the second stage saw Gino Bartali crash after hitting a dog, Bartali dislocating his elbow in the process. Ignoring medical advice to quit the race, Bartali continued despite losing time. It paved the way for his *gregario* (*see domestique*, Chapter Three), Fausto Coppi, to take centre stage and win his first Grand Tour.

More recently, Sandy Casar (2007) and Philippe Gilbert (2012) have been among the Tour riders taken out by dogs running into the road. Cesar survived and went on to dust himself down and win the stage; Gilbert ended up having to be pulled away from a confrontation with the dog's owner by his team manager. 'There was nothing we could do to avoid it,' Gilbert told the media after the stage. 'I was pretty upset at the people because I think it's very dangerous to leave such a big dog running into the bunch. It could have been really bad.' If Gilbert knows his cycling history, he will be aware of one particularly tragic case: during the 1984 Tour of the Algarve, the Portuguese rider Joaquim Agostino crashed into a dog 200 metres before the finish. Initially seeming okay, it later transpired that Agostino had fractured his skull in the crash; he fell into a coma and died ten days later.

If dogs are the most dangerous animals to avoid, a wary cyclist should also be on the lookout for horses and cattle. At both the 1975 and 2000 Tours, a horse has got so excited by the passing peloton that it couldn't resist the urge to jump the fence and join in the fun. Back in 1909, race leader François Faber was both knocked off his bicycle by a horse, and had his bike kicked away by the animal for good measure.

Cattle tend to be a bit more slow moving, but are not without their problems. In the 1920s, Gustav van Slembrouck was taken out of the Tour of Flanders by a reversing cow. At the 2015 Tour de France, Warren Barguil narrowly escaped disaster heading down the Col du Tourmalet at close to 90 kilometres per hour when a herd of cattle decided to check if the grass was greener on the other side. He was luckier that Mikel Landa in the 2013 Criterium du Dauphiné – he hit a cow that walked onto the road and had to abandon the race with a broken collarbone.

ROAD FURNITURE

A somewhat clunky phrase to describe the ever-growing accoutrements of traffic-calming measures placed on the road in the form of traffic islands, sleeping policemen, bollards and what have you. Great for slowing down drivers; less great if you're a cyclist crashing into them at full speed.

Road furniture is less of an issue in the bigger races, where firstly, the size of the race dictates that most of the roads need to be above a certain size for the peloton and *caravane* to pass through and, secondly, there's the money and planning available to remove the worst offenders in time for the race. Slightly lower down the race pecking order, however, the limited cash involved can either mean that road furniture can't be removed, or that the requisite steward with a whistle and red flag to warn the riders is missing.

That was the case at the end of the second stage of the 2016 Tour of Qatar, where an unmarked road island took out a number of riders sprinting for the line. At the finish of the first stage of the 2015 Tour of the Basque Country, riders came across two metre-high metal poles, a metre and a half into the road, in the run up to the line. The organizers had decided that putting a traffic cone on top of each pole was probably sufficient: the young British rider Adam Yates broke a finger in the subsequent crash; the American Peter Stetine broke his tibia, patella and four ribs.

Sometimes it is not just riders who get injured in the collisions. At the 2014 Tour of Flanders, a spectator was stood watching the race on a traffic island in the middle of the road. While most of the peloton managed to peel around the island, the Garmin-Sharp rider Johan Vansummeren hit both the island and the spectator standing there.

Roundabouts are not strictly road furniture, but can produce their own problems if a rider doesn't get their line right. On a wet fifth day of the 2014 Tour de France, Chris Froome was among a number of riders to crash on the early roundabouts and ended up abandoning. Even if crashing isn't a problem, going the wrong way round can leave you losing position. At the 2011 Vuelta, the sixteenth stage to Haro saw the riders hit a large roundabout 300 metres before the finish. The race route was to go left, the cars were to peel right; but the Leopard Trek lead-out train at the front of the race was uncertain which way to go and splintered in both directions. Just what you need when you've ridden 200 kilometres in the Spanish heat.

COBBLES
Pavé (Fr)

'When it's wet they're a death slide,' says Geraint Thomas in *The World of Cycling According to G*. 'When it's dry they're a dust storm. They shake you like an earthquake, rattle your bones, loosen your eyes from their sockets.' And yet for

so many cyclists, riding on cobbles is one of cycling's most daunting and exciting challenges. 'On my Roubaix debut it felt like I was holding a jackhammer and trying to break the road beneath me,' Geraint Thomas remembers. 'I loved it.'

They're a road surface synonymous with the northern Classics: the cobbled hills of the Tour of Flanders; the Kemmelberg of Gent–Wevelgem; and of course the many *secteurs* of Paris–Roubaix, from Orchies to the Forest of Arenberg. Indeed, for the original Paris–Roubaix back in 1896, the entire final 60 kilometres was over *pavé*. And not just nice, neat, well-made little stones either. That they were nicknamed 'bowler hats' give some indication of the size of the cobbles en route. Indeed, one of the Dutch terms for cobblestones is the somewhat macabre *kinderkopje* or 'children's heads'.

They're not a road surface to be attempted on a rider's usual bike: these are days for thicker tyres at a lower pressure and extra tape on the handlebars. And don't hold on too tight: 'the worst thing you can do is to grab hold of the bars tighter or tense your whole upper body,' Paris–Roubaix podium finisher Roger Hammond told RoadCyclingUK.com in an interview. 'Float rather than bounce,' advises Geraint Thomas in his memoir. To ride well on the cobbles requires a unique combination of confidence, skill and luck.

If you haven't got any of those, it's probably best to get off and walk before the *pavé* fling you off. In Ridley Scott's famous 1970s Hovis advert, the then state of British cycling was summed up by the baker's boy pushing, not riding, his bike up the cobbled hill that was meant to be Yorkshire, but was in fact Gold Hill in Shaftesbury, Dorset. Bread delivered, his questionable descending skills were little better – legs out of the pedals in a star shape were asking for him to be upended. Feeble stuff: a successor to Louison Bobet (nicknamed The Baker of Saint Meen because of his father's profession), he was not.

PROTESTS

With between 1.5 and four billion people watching the Tour de France annually – depending on which set of statistics you believe – it is inevitable that over the years different interest groups have attempted to interrupt the race to publicize their particular causes.

In 1982, for example, striking French steelworkers disrupted a number of stages. One was rerouted through a steelworks to avoid confrontation; another was blocked by Usinor workers at Denain and the stage was cancelled, a first for the race. In 1988 it was the turn of shipyard workers from Saint-Nazaire; in 1990 it was French sheep farmers, with race organizers guiding the race along back roads on the hoof to avoid the demonstration. In 2003, protesters demonstrating about the imprisonment of anti-globalization agitator José Bové, brought the race to a halt; in 2016, winemakers threatened protests after the Tour did a sponsorship deal with Cono Sur, a Chilean wine manufacturer.

As well as striking workers, Grand Tours have also been the target of terrorist organizations, in particular the Basque separatists ETA who have targeted both the Tour and the Vuelta over the years. In 1967, ETA covered the descent of the Sollube with nails and oil, causing numerous crashes and punctures. At the following year's Vuelta, they detonated a bomb on the Puerto de Urbasa: no riders were hurt and at the organizers insistence, the race continued, with the riders carrying their bikes over the rubble. At the prologue of the 1992 Tour de France in San Sebastian, a bomb was found underneath the car of commentator Phil Liggett; in 1997, when the Tour reached Pamplona, police had to make safe a four-kilogram bomb left in a bin.

It's debatable what would have happened if Bernard Hinault had ever got hold of a terrorist trying to interrupt the race, but you can probably guess. When striking dockers from La Ciotat tried to block the 1984 Paris–Nice, Hinault steamed straight into them, punching the protestors. Years later, he'd lost none of his fire, shoving another protestor off the winner's podium at the 2008 Tour de France.

MOTO RIDERS

They shouldn't be a problem, really. And yet the number of cyclists getting knocked off by one of the many moto riders buzzing around the peloton seems to grow race by race, season by season. Jakob Fuglsang (Tour de France, 2015), Greg Van Avermaet (Classic San Sebastian, 2015), Peter Sagan (Vuelta, 2015), Sergio Paulihno (Vuelta, 2015), Stig Broeckx (Kuurne–Brussels–Kuurne, 2016) and Antoine Demoite (Gent-Wevelgem, 2016) are just some of the more recent examples; the latter tragically dying from his injuries. It's not just moto riders, of course – Jonny Hoogerland was famously taken out by a media car at the 2011 Tour de France – but the accidents involving larger vehicles are fewer and further between.

There can be a lot of motorbikes following a race: many are media in the form of TV, radio and photographers, but there are also the *ardoisier*, police bikes, neutral support bikes, *commissaires* and what have you. All riders have to hold a UCI license, including the media since 2013, and there are plenty of rules about how moto riders shouldn't hinder the progress of cyclists. But in a race situation, things aren't always as simple as they seem in the rulebook. Moto rider Luke Evans, interviewed by *Cycling Weekly* in 2015, argued that every situation is complicated: 'You might say that the cyclist is always in the right, and that it's our job to stay out of their way at all times — but that is often not possible in the tight, fluid and sometimes chaotic environment directly in front and especially behind the race. And inside the race too, as we often have to pass the peloton in very tight situations. You can be minding your own business and still find yourself trying to avoid a crash or a rider suddenly changing direction.'

One can argue, as some have, that the number of motorbikes following a race should be reduced. But equally, media coverage is the lifeblood of the sport – take that away and its reach to the world at large is reduced. And the media form only part of the swarm of motorbikes: reducing the number of, say, *commissaires*, leaves the way open for unwatched riders to take a 'swig' from a 'sticky bottle'. After Tinkoff-Saxo lost two of its riders at the 2015 Vuelta, it suggested a raft of changes to the rules, one of which was for the minimum distance allowed between a motorbike and a rider to be increased from five to ten metres. But is this enforceable on a tight, narrow mountain road? This is a debate that will run and run.

TACKS

In terms of ways to sabotage a bicycle race, sometimes the simplest are still the best. Covering the road with drawing pins, carpet tacks or nails is a long-established pastime, and while the bikes themselves have transformed over the decades, the way to stop remains resolutely, almost quaintly, old fashioned.

Nails and tacks were a problem right from the start of the Tour de France. At the 1905 Tour, there was an estimated 125 kilograms of nails spread across the road on the stage between Paris and Nancy: such saboteurs were known as *les semeurs des clous* or 'nail sowers'. Over a century on, and saboteurs and protesters were again spreading nails on the routes of the 2011 Giro di Padania and 2012 Tour de France. The reasons for such action vary. Back in the day, this behaviour was sometimes the preserve of fans of particular cyclists, trying to stop their rivals catching up; sometimes it is mindless vandalism; and sometimes it is deployed by NIMBY locals who don't want a cycling race coming through their region.

This has certainly been the case with sportives in the UK in recent years. Events in the New Forest and also the Étape Caledonia in Scotland have seen nails, tacks, drawing pins, screws and staples deposited on the road. At the 2014 Valley Vélo Sportive in South Wales, more than 70 riders punctured because of drawing pins on the road: pins that the person responsible had gone to the lengths of painting black so that they weren't visible on the road surface, and had positioned on a sharp descent when riders were travelling at 70 kilometres per hour.

WIND

Wind. It can be a rider's friend if it's a tailwind – allowing them to feel like they're Superman. It can be an enemy if it's a headwind, slowing riders down in a way that never quite seems fair. And if it's a crosswind, then it can cause havoc, with the peloton splitting up into echelons (*see* Chapter Two) to take full advantage or just survive. Over the course of a day's racing, a route can lead the riders in all sort of directions. As Geraint Thomas says in his memoir, 'Wind is sly. It pretends it's not there and then you turn a corner or pedal past a building and – slap! It blows the race and all your careful plans apart.'

Some places are notorious for their wind: La Mancha in Spain is known for its crosswinds and as *Viva La Vuelta!* notes, 'the history of the Vuelta is littered with race favourites who have fallen foul of the winds of Castilla.' The Tour of Qatar is another race known for its wind. Experienced riders jockey for position from the off, in anticipation of the echelons that are inevitably going to follow. The Netherlands, with its flat terrain and exposure to the sea, can get pretty gusty and is one of the reasons why the Dutch are often good riders in the wind. Then there's Mont Ventoux – one of the various theories about the origins of its name is that it derives from *venteux*, meaning 'windy'. Certainly it's blowy at the summit: gusts of 150 miles per hour have been recorded and the wind *averages* over 90 kilometres per hour for about two-thirds of the year.

There hasn't been such a storm during a cycling race, but other races have undoubtedly been hit by strong winds. Such was the strength of the gusts at the 2015 Gent–Wevelgem, that Gert Steegman, Edvald Boasson Hagen and Geraint Thomas were among those blown off the road and into canals, wooden posts and ditches, respectively. The remnants of storm Xynthia blew apart the 2010 Kuurne–Brussels–Kuurne, with just 26 riders finishing, and signage from the finish having to be removed in case it blew away. At the third stage of the 2016 Volta a La Marina in Spain, the riders didn't even get out of the neutralized zone before the race was abandoned because of hurricane winds: such was the force of the headwinds that riders found themselves stationary at best and falling over at worst.

SNOW

Sometimes it Snows in April goes the Prince song. His Purpleness had obviously not been paying close attention to road racing, where snow can also make a rider's life a misery in May, June and beyond.

There aren't as many great snowy cycling stories from the present era, as *commissaires* tend to neutralize or cancel stages to avoid the worst. In 2013, however, snowy weather led to the shortening of the Milan–San Remo, and the cancellation of one stage and the neutering of the queen stage of the Giro. Equally, snow, fog and ice created confusion on the road during the 2014 Giro stage when Nairo Quintana took the *maglia rosa* (*see* Chapter Five).

Being earlier in the season than the other Grand Tours, the Giro is the race with the most dramatic snow stories. At the 1956 Giro, Charley Gaul started stage 16 in twenty-fourth place, but raced through a blizzard to reach the summit of the Bordone first by eight minutes (the previous *maglia rosa*, meanwhile, hid in a farmhouse). Three decades later, the 1988 Giro took the riders over the Gavia in blizzard conditions – the descent reduced some riders to tears, saw Johan van der Velde pull up at the first hairpin and lose 48 minutes on the stage, and Andy Hampsten slither his way to race victory.

It's not just the Giro that can be affected by snow. The 2013 Vuelta had its own flurries over the top of the Envalira: 14 riders abandoned. At the 1909 Tour, François Faber battled through snow and pretty much all the elements to win the race. And then, of course there are the Classics, most famously Neige–Bastogne–Neige (see Chapter Fourteen).

TECHNICAL SECTIONS

One phrase that seems to be used with increasing frequency in cycling

BESPOKE

commentary is the description of a race section as 'technical'. 'This is a very tricky, technical descent', for example. Or 'a really technical finish' for the riders here. Essentially, and this might be being slightly unfair, 'technical' means that there are some corners involved. So rather than bombing down a nice straight downhill descent, the riders have to navigate a number of hairpins. Or rather than a nice wide promenade to take the race all the way to the finish line, there are a couple of pesky corners thrown into the *parcours* for the rider to cope with. A technical route requires a rider to pay attention rather than putting their head down: a smart rider will have looked at the roadbook (*see* Chapter Nine) in advance to work out which racing lines to take, when to slam the brakes on, and the requisite moment to attack.

CRASHES
Chute (Fr)/*Caduta* (It)

Cyclists crash. Repeatedly. An informal rider survey carried out by Jens Voigt at the 2012 Tour de France suggested that 75 per cent of the riders had fallen off at some point between the prologue and the Champs-Élysées sprint finish.

Crashes can occur for any number of reasons – a difficult road surface or tricky weather conditions – but equally, a crash can simply be down to human error: a touched wheel here, someone not paying attention there. In 2019, Chris Froome crashed on a reconnaissance ride when a freak gust of wind caught his bike while he was trying to blow his nose. During a race, a single rider going down can have significant consequences for those around them: a peloton in full flight can be up to 200 riders packed in at speeds of 80 kilometres per hour. If you're in the middle and someone goes over, then the chances are that you're going to go over, too.

In *The Racer,* David Millar describes being involved in one of the largest Tour de France pile-ups of recent times – stage 6 of the 2012 Tour. 'First there was the noise: metal and carbon grinding and smashing, tyres skidding, brakes screeching. Then there were the impacts. I started seeing them from a long way out: bikes and bodies were going everywhere... there was zero hope of escaping it, so then it became a case of braking as hard as you could and rubbing as much speed as possible before the impact... once your crash is completed you are at the mercy of those careening in from behind... the best thing to do is to cover your face and close your eyes.'

Major crashes often tend to happen in three places: on the opening week of Grand Tours; in the Classics; and as the peloton are approaching a sprint finish. Each of these scenarios has two things in common – the numbers of riders involved and the tension of the teams. In a Classics race, positioning can be everything, which results in a lot of jockeying and fighting for position at the front; the same is true of a sprint finish. The first week of a Tour sees a similar state of nervousness, not helped by the fact that the opening stages tend to be in the north rather than the south of France, so often take place in poorer weather conditions. Again, there is that desire to sit at the front: the sprint teams want to be there to control the flat stages; the GC teams want to keep their contenders out of harm's way. By the later stages of the Tour, the weather tends to be better, the peloton tends to be smaller, and the riders tend to be more relaxed. The big crashes, tend to ease off.

Although such pile-ups make for unpleasant viewing and are horrible to be part of, those large crashes don't tend to cause life-threatening injuries. Of the riders who have died from crashes in major races, their tragic deaths have usually resulted from leaving the road (Francesco Cepeda, Fabio Casartelli), or hitting something as they went down (Wouter Weyland). Once you're off the road, you're in the lap of the Gods. In 1951, the yellow jersey wearer Wim Van Est crashed on the Aubisque; falling down the side of the mountain, he ended up on a narrow ledge, which saved his life. But a small group of other riders, tragically, have not been so lucky.

Below A touch of wheels at
the 1979 Tour de France

TEN | Nicknames

Cycling has a strong tradition of giving its riders nicknames: right from the start it was seen as adding a romanticism and heroism to their exploits. And while the Anglicized presence in the peloton has seen the growth of less exciting abbreviated monikers – Wiggo, Cav, G, Froomey – there are plenty in the peloton still doing their bit to hold up the old traditions.

LE PETIT RAMONEUR (FR)
The Little Chimney Sweep

A number of riders in the early days of competition racing got their names from their profession. Lucien Pothier, who finished second in the original Tour de France was known as the Butcher of Sens, not because he had a reputation for carving up his opponents, but because he was from Sens and his profession was, well, you've probably guessed... Julio Jimenez, who came second in the 1967 Tour, was known as The Watchmaker of Avila, because, well, you're good at this aren't you? And the first winner of the Tour de France, Maurice Garin, was *Le Petit Ramoneur* on account of being five foot three and his ability to sweep up a breakaway. Not really. He cleaned chimneys.

IL SCOIATTOLO DEI NAVIGLI (IT)
The Squirrel of the Canals

There is a short but curious history of squirrel nicknames in cycling. In the noughties, Chris Boardman and his team of marginal gains experimenters at

British Cycling called themselves the Secret Squirrel Club (*see also* Marginal Gains, Chapter Thirteen). 'I spent a few hours messing around on the computer and created a logo,' Boardman recalled in his memoir: 'a silhouetted squirrel whose outline was filled with the union flag. When I showed it to the team, one of them pointed out that the squirrel I'd used was Canadian.' When Jonathan Boyer became the first American rider to take part in the Tour de France in 1981, his vegetarian diet along, with the nuts and fruit he stashed in his cycling jersey, raised eyebrows among the peloton: 'Enter the Squirrel' records the The Handmade Cylist's *Miscellany of le Tour de France*.

But the original *scoiattoli* can be traced back to the beginnings of the sport in the form of Italian cyclist Carlo Galetti. Galetti won the 1910 Giro and went by the name of *il Scoiattolo dei Navigli* – The Squirrel of the Canals. Which might seem a slightly odd nickname – squirrels and canals not usually going together – but this is a nickname of two halves.The 'squirrel' element came from Galetti's lightness, nimbleness and bushy red tail (okay, possibly not the latter); the 'canals' bit was because Galetti hailed from the Milanese suburb of Corsico, famous for its water network. So it's The Squirrel of the Canals in the same way that Nibali is The Shark of the Straits (*see below*).

THE DEATH RIDER OF LICHTERVELDE
Den Doodrijder Van Lichtervelde (Dutch)
Now, that's more like a nickname. The Death Rider of Lichtervelde was the Flandrian Henri Van Leerberghe, who won the Tour of Flanders in 1919. Van Leerberghe, a former soldier, was proper Flandrian-tough and got his nickname, according to Peter Cossins, 'because he used to tell his rivals he would ride them into an early grave or would die trying.'

He rode to victory in the Ronde despite having only a single-speed bike and coming up against a train that blocked his path at a level crossing once he'd broken clear. As with Henri Pélissier at Paris–Roubaix a few weeks later, Van Leerberghe picked up his bicycle, boarded the train, walked down the carriage and climbed down the other side to carry on. Legend has it that he crossed the finish line with a bottle of beer in his hand.

THE HERON
Il Airone (It)
Fausto Coppi, as befits one of cycling's giants, had a number of nicknames. Such was his success that the term *il campionissimo* ('champion of champions') passed to him and stuck. But perhaps the most appropriate nickname is the one that reflects his physique and cycling style: *Il Airone*, or The Heron.

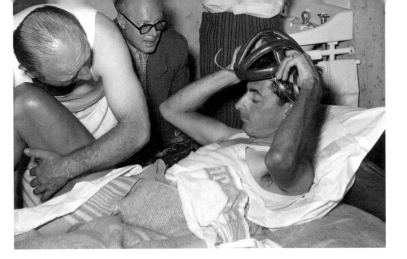
Above A massage from Biagio
Cavanna for *il Airone*: Fausto Coppi
at the 1951 Tour de France

A sighting of a heron riding a bike has yet to be recorded, but you can only assume that if you did see one, they'd be a bit like Fausto Coppi. In his book *Tour de France*, Graham Fife describes Coppi's physique as, '5'10", ten and a half stone, long spindly legs, hunched scrawny shoulders, disproportionately small torso, handsome aqualine features with a long beak of a nose and high cheekbones.' Like a heron on land, Coppi was awkward and ungainly. Once in flight on his bike, however, the man was poetry in motion.

In *Fallen Angel*, William Fotheringham quotes the Italian writer Orio Vergani, who 'coined a phrase now synonymous with [Coppi's] death, "the great heron closing his wings."'

LE PÉDALLEUR DE CHARME (FR)

It would take a special sort of rider to become the first non-Italian winner of the Giro D'Italia. But it would taking a special and charming rider to do without gaining the wrath of the *tifosi*.

At the 1950 Giro D'Italia, a crash for Fausto Coppi left his pelvis broken in three places. The stage seemed set for Coppi's great rival, Gino Bartali to win the title and, with the race concluding in Rome, to enjoy an audience with the Pope. But Bartali didn't factor in the form of Swiss rider Hugo Koblet, or the fact that Coppi ordered his *gregari* to help Koblet and thwart his rival.

To begin with, Koblet cycled to a soundtrack of boos and whistles. But as the race continued he won the Italians over with his charm and good looks as he claimed the title. The following year, he won the Tour de France by a huge 22 minutes, leading to *L'Équipe* hailing him 'Apollo on a bike' and singer Jacques Grello calling him '*le pédalleur de charme*'.

Koblet was style personified. Of his riding style, *L'Équipe* said he 'rode harmoniously, with suppleness, his elbows with a slight outward flex, his arms absorbing the vibrations coming up the road.' Keeping up appearances, Koblet always had a comb and a bottle of eau de cologne with him while cycling. In the winter of 1951, he was invited to go to Mexico by their cycling federation, not to take part in their race, but to ride half an hour ahead to cheers from the crowd, and then hand out the prizes at the end of each stage.

THE EAGLE OF TOLEDO
El Aguila del Toledo (Sp)

There are enough cyclists named after birds to fill an aviary. As well as Coppi's Heron, there's Paolo Salvodelli (The Falcon), Iban Mayo (The Rooster), Robert Gesink (The Condor of Varsseveld), David Moncoutie (*Moncoucou* – The Cuckoo), and Fabio Parra (The Condor of the Andes), to name just a few. Then there are all the various eagles: Thierry Claveyrolat (The Eagle of Vizille), Marcel Kint (The Black Eagle), Bjarne Riis (The Eagle of Herning) and Harm Ottenbros (The Eagle of Hoogerheide).

But none of these eagle-eyed cyclists match up to Federico Bahamontes, The Eagle of Toledo. Bahamontes was so called for his ability to fly up mountains and was one of the greatest climbers ever to grace the sport. This nickname stuck, but it's worth noting that during his early cycling career, he was known by some slightly less salubrious terms. Growing up, he worked as a hired hand at Toledo market and become known as *El Lechuga* – The Lettuce Boy, which somehow doesn't have quite the same romantic ring as The Eagle... Within the peloton, Bahamontes was also known for selling goods to the other riders: he 'had an entire shop in his suitcase' according to one rider and, 'would only take cash, no credit.' This behaviour – a hangover from Bahamontes' tough start in life – soon gave him a reputation and the somewhat un-PC nickname, *el Gitano* – the Gypsy.

MONSIEUR CHRONO (FR)

Does a nickname affect performance? Take the early 1960s battle between the French riders Jacques Anquetil and Raymond Poulidor. Would you put your money on *Monsieur Chrono* or Pou-Pou? So called because of his time-trialling skills, Anquetil sounded similarly authoritative in the guise of his alternative nickname, *Maître Jacques*, whereas Poulidor was more commonly known as The Eternal Second.

RIK I/RIK II

CAMPAGNOLO

ANQUETIL
64

Great Belgian riders called Rik. They're like buses, etc... If only there was some way of telling them apart...

Rik I was Henri 'Rik' Van Steenbergen and a phenomenal one-day rider: he won the World title three times as well as eight Classics, including Milan–San Remo, the Tour of Flanders (twice), and Paris–Roubaix (also twice). In his first Paris–Roubaix victory in 1948, he also secured the *Ruben Jaune* – the award for the fastest average speed in a Classic race. In his second victory in 1952, he beat Fausto Coppi in an epic battle on cobbles. Rik I raced anywhere and everywhere, as long as the money was good. It is estimated that such was his thirst for racing and ability to win that he won just over 1300 races during his career.

Following hot on his heels was Rik Van Looy – Rik II. In 1958, Rik I heard Rik II described on the radio as 'the best in the world'. He psyched himself up for one last hurrah, riding 1000 kilometres in a week to prepare for Flèche–Wallonne, where he duly beat his younger rival. But after that, it was Rik II's time. Van Looy's *palmarés* are no less impressive than Van Steenbergen's: yes, he had just the two World Titles rather than three (though he finished runner-up twice), but he also won every Monument, including the Tour of Flanders twice and Paris–Roubaix three times, not to mention five Tour stages, six Giro stages and eighteen Vuelta ones. He then passed the baton on to Eddy Merckx, unhelpfully not called Rik, to complete a remarkable period in Belgian cycling.

THE YORKSHIRE HAUSFRAU

Women's cycling does not generally have as rich a seam of nicknames as the men's sport: a point illustrated by the fact that Marianne Vos's moniker is the 'Cannibal' or the 'Female Merckx' for those to whom the point is not already obvious enough. Rather than being celebrated for her own achievements, her success is apparently best made sense of with by reference to her male predecessors.

Beryl Burton, – by some margin the greatest British female cyclist of all time and one of the great female cyclists, and great British cyclists, full stop – acquired her own nickname through her German rivals. In the UK, Burton's success was rampant: 70 national titles over a remarkable 25- year period; a record for the 12-hour time-trial that she broke in 1967 and which still stands today – a record she achieved while overtaking the male champion Mike McNamara and offering him a Liquorice Allsort as she sped past.

Internationally, she had a range of rainbow jerseys to go with her wardrobe of national ones: five golds on the track, two as world road race champion. But this was the 1960s and at the height of the Cold War, when Russian and East German athletes had the sort of, ahem, medical support that was meant to ensure success. So what was Beryl's secret? A team was despatched to Yorkshire to discover her magic formula. As Suze Clemitson describes in *Ride the Revolution*, 'it turned out Beryl's PED [performance enhancing drug] of choice was hard graft and rhubarb.'

THE CANNIBAL

The most famous nickname for the most famous rider in cycling history was the work of a twelve-year-old schoolgirl.

In 1969, Eddy Merckx dominated the Tour de France. He didn't just win the *maillot jeune*, but bagged the points jersey and King of the Mountains competition to boot. A few days before the end of the Tour, Merckx's teammate at Peugeot, Christian Raymond, was visited by his wife and daughter, Brigitte. Interviewed by Daniel Friebe for his biography on Eddy Merckx, Raymond recalled that, 'my daughter asked me why Merckx always had to

win and I tried to explain that it was normal, because he was the best rider. She went quiet for a minute, then looked at me quizzically and said, "well then, he's a real cannibal..." I liked that name... and mentioned it to a couple of journalists that day. They, evidently, liked it too.'

A few years earlier, when Merckx turned professional and rode for Rik Van Looy's Solo-Superia team, he was known as 'Jack Palance', on account of his passing resemblance to the American actor. And while The Cannibal is the nickname that has stuck over the years, it was not the only name he was known by as his career continued. In Italy, he was known as *il mostro* – The Monster. Many riders also called him The Crocodile.

THE BADGER
Le Blaireau (Fr)

'A badger is a beautiful thing,' Bernard Hinault told *L'Équipe* in 2003. 'When sWit's hunted, it goes into its sett and waits. When it comes out again, it attacks. That's the reason for my nickname. When I'm annoyed I go home, you don't see me for a month. When I come out again, I win. You attack me; I get my claws out.'

As with Eddy Merckx's nickname, Hinault's moniker captures something about the raw drive of this rider, and his desire and determination to win. The name originally came from Maurice Le Guilloux and Bernard Talbourdet, who trained with Hinault early in his career and called him *blaireau* (The Badger) in a vain attempt to take their young colleague down a peg or two. When the term was overheard by Pierre Chany, the esteemed French cycling writer, he seized upon it and the name stuck.

In his biography of Bernard Hinault, William Fotheringham suggests that the nickname worked so well, not just because of the way that Hinault rode, but also because of a passing resemblance and, more importantly, its nod towards Hinault's country roots. You can take the man out of Brittany, but you can't take Brittany out of the man.

THE YOYO

Some nicknames focus on a cyclist's appearance and not always in a flattering way. The Australian Phil Anderson was known as Dr Teeth, on account of his prominent set of dentures. Laurent Jalabert was called The Panda, because of the rings around his eyes. In fact, think of any facial feature and there will be a rider with an unflattering nickname linked to it: Ferdinand Kübler was known as The Nose due to his sizeable conk; Antonio Belvilacqua was Big Lips; Maurice

Archambaud was Chubby Cheeks; Pierre Brambilla, Clogface (because of his big chin); Marco Pantani, *Elefantino* (Big Ears, Dumbo). Ah, peloton banter.

In a sport obsessed by weight, it is perhaps inevitable that anyone a half-inch wider than a stick insect might get some abuse. The Belgian rider Philippe Thys might have had three Tour de France victories on his *palmarès* but it didn't stop him being known as Fat Dog, on account of the thickness of this thighs and his low riding style. And then there was Jan Ullrich, a rider notorious for putting on the pounds during the off-season and then shedding them again in advance of the Tour de France. So although he liked to be known as *Der Kaiser*, it is perhaps the nickname The Yoyo that stuck a little bit more.

THE PIRATE
Il Pirata (It)

Marco Pantani wasn't always known as *Il Pirata* – The Pirate. Originally the peloton called him either *Elefantino* (because of his Dumbo-style big ears) or Nosferatu, on account of his face. Nice. But as he grew in stature as a rider, so he shed these names for one based on his new trademark look: earring, bandana, goatee. The Pirate nickname emerged around 1997 (it is suggested that the bandana came about because he couldn't get a cycling cap to fit his head), but who came up with the nickname and the piratical element depends on who you listen to. Certainly, it captured the swashbuckling element of his riding style as well – out for adventure, taking a risk, and making his riders walk the plank. Okay, maybe not the last one.

Pantani isn't the only Italian rider to reach for the sea for inspiration. Vincenzo Nibali, when he is not being called Nibbles, is the self-styled Shark from the Straits. To be fair to Nibali, he comes from Messina, on the coast opposite Sicily, where there are indeed sharks in the water. And like Pantani, the nickname also reflects his attacking riding style. Nibali even has a shark-themed bike, with eyes and teeth on the frame, if not a fin on his back, presumably for aerodynamic reasons.

EL PISTOLERO (SP)

Alberto Contador's original nickname when he started cycling was 'Pantani', because of his climbing ability. But as he became a professional, he needed a nickname all of his own, hence *El Pistolero de Pinto*, to give him his full title (Pinto is the small town near Madrid where Contador was born).

As nicknames go, Contador is not alone in reaching for a bit of metaphorical firepower: Alejandro Valverde goes by the nickname *El Bala* or The Bullet (or sometime *El Balaverde*, The Green Bullet, if you're feeling colourful). Then there is the Manx Missile (Mark Cavendish); Raphaël Géminiani, *le Grand Fusil* (Top Gun); and Giuseppo Saronni, whose World Championship-winning attack at Goodwood was compared to a rifle-shot. But Contador is the only one to have a signature pistol-firing salute as he passes the finishing line.

Or is it a pistol? Interviewed in *Bicycling* magazine in 2011, Contador explained that the salute had a different origin: 'My friends, they said, you don't ever do anything when you win. So I decided to do something. So I do this [*points to his heart*]. I believe in my friends and in my family. When I win, I do this. This is for you. It is not a gun. It's for you. After, "the *Pistolero*." [*makes a face*] For a long time, I say it's not, it's not the *Pistolero*, then, eventually, OK, fine. OK, it's *Pistolero*!'

PURITO (SP)

Spanish for a small cigar. This is the nickname ascribed to Joachim Rodriguez after an incident when he was a freshly turned professional and out for a training ride with his ONCE team. Showing an early example of the climbing skills that he would become famous for, Rodriguez dropped such illustrious teammates as Abraham Olano and Carlos Sastre on a climb. Not content with leaving it at that, Rodriguez proceeded to rub salt into the proceedings by miming smoking a cigar as he rode away.

Determined to put their upstart teammate in his place, the other riders told Rodriguez that in return for such insolence, he had to smoke a cigar at dinner in front of Manolo Saiz, the team's disciplinarian boss. Rather than chastening Rodriguez, he sat down at dinner with his *purito* and did precisely that. A nickname was born.

THE BUTTERFLY OF MAASTRICHT

Not exactly the sort of nickname to strike the fear of God into rival riders, the Butterfly of Maastricht is the moniker of Dutch rider Tom Dumoulin, the World Champion time-trialling specialist turned surprise Grand Tour contender. He was unlucky not to win the Vuelta in 2015, but went on to win the Giro in 2017.

The nickname, which Dumoulin apparently doesn't like, is one that has stuck since his junior days. It comes from the elegance of his riding style: as one Dutch journalist put it, he could 'ride a time-trial in a dinner jacket and cross the line without his bow-tie being out of place.' In Dutch, the word for a bow-tie is a butterfly-tie, and it is from this that the nickname apparently derives, rather than him being some sort of secret lepidopterist.

ELEVEN | Montagnes

'The hills are alive… ', Julie Andrews almost once sang, 'with the sound of drunk Dutch cycling fans cheering the race leaders up the mountainside.' In this chapter, in a variety of gradients, the only way is up.

HORS CATÉGORIE OR HC (FR)
Categorìa Especial or ESP (Sp)/Without Category

Originally in the Grand Tours, mountains weren't ranked at all. Then in the 1930s, the Giro and Tour both introduced climbing competitions. To begin with, points were awarded according to a rider's position over the top of the climb, but some mountains were bigger than others and a system of grading them needed to be created. Mountains in the Tour were divided into two, then three, then four categories over the following decades.

According to urban legend, the categorization of the Tour mountains was originally down to which gear was needed to get up the slope if you were driving in a Citroën 2CV. The truth is that there was a slightly less interesting calculation involving the average gradient of the slope and the length of the climb. But even this wasn't mathematically accurate: a mountain could be assigned a different category depending on whether it appeared towards the start or end of the day. There's a sense, too, of whether a mountain 'feels' like it belongs to a certain category.

It's not an exact science by any means; a point underlined by the introduction of a new top category in 1979 – *Hors Catégorie* (HC), meaning beyond or without categorization. Putting aside the semantics of whether one can categorize something that is uncategorizable, this was a way of creating a new 'super' category of the hardest mountains, shunting everything else down a 'cat' in the process. (A bit like the introduction of the Premier League in English football in the early 1990s, with the old Division Two renamed Division One and so forth.)

Since 1979, there have been getting on for 40 different HC climbs used in the Tour. Some are well known – Alpe d'Huez, Galibier, Ventoux – while others have had occasional visits.

At the Vuelta, the equivalent of an HC climb is a *Categorìa Especial* (ESP). By contrast, the Giro d'Italia has so far resisted any mountain classification inflation, sticking to ranking its mountains in an old money one-to-four system.

LE CERCLE DU MORT (FR)
The Circle of Death

'The Tour de France only became the Tour de France when we sent the riders into the mountains,' Henri Desgrange, originator of the Tour, once famously said. The year Desgrange decided to send them there was 1910, at the behest of his assistant race director Alphonses Steinès, who recommended that the race go to the Pyrenees.

Desgranges sent Steinès to suss out the potential route, a journey that Steinès was not wholly straight about when reporting to his boss. Scouting the Tourmalet, Steinès' car got stuck on the unmade roads in the snow. He ended up making it to the summit on foot, though not without having to be rescued from a fall into a ravine in the process. So the telegram he sent to Desgrange on his descent was not an entirely accurate description of what he discovered: 'Tourmalet crossed STOP very good road STOP perfectly practicable STOP Steinès.'

Stage 10 of that year's race featured four Pyrenean climbs for the first time, all of which have since become firm fixtures on the Tour: the Peyresourde, Aspin, Tourmalet and Aubisque. The Col de Peyresourde (1560 metres) has featured over 50 times on the Tour and is a climb of 815 metres at an average gradient of 7.4 per cent. The Col d'Aspin (1489 metres), is a 775-metre climb at an average of 6.3 per cent. It has been included on the Tour's itinerary over 60 times. The Col du Tourmalet (2115 metres) is either a 1400- or 1250-metre climb, depending on whether you're approaching from the west of east side; both have an average gradient of about 7.4 per cent. Finally the Col d'Ausbique (1709 metres) is a 1225 metre climb at a misleading average of 4.2 per cent (misleading because there are flats and descents along the way).

Above Eddy Merckx climbs the Col du Tourmalet at the 1969 Tour de France

Over the years, these four mountains have became known as the 'circle of death' – a moniker applied by Jean Robic, who won the 1947 stage over these four climbs. Death was also on the minds of the cyclists attempting the ride for the first time back in 1910. Reaching the top of the Aubisque, Octave Lapize famously shouted 'You are all assassins!' at the *commissaires*. 'No human being should be put through an ordeal like that.'

Unfortunately for Robic and his fellow riders, the Peyresourde–Aspin–Tourmalet–Aubisque combo has become a firm favourite on the Tour route. In 1969, it was the scene of one of Eddy Merckx's most famous rides: he broke clear on the slopes of the Tourmalet and stayed out in front for the stage's remaining 140 kilometres, beating the next placed rider by eight minutes. This led to the famous 'MERCKXISSIMO' headline and certainly, to take the honours across these Pyrenean peaks is an undeniable show of strength.

MOUNTAIN PASSES
Passo (It)
Some iconic climbs are known by the name of their mountain, Mont this or Col that. Others are all about the peak – the Alto in Alto d'Angliru emphasizing its height. But just as some travelers know it's all about the journey rather than the destination, some of the greatest climbs are all about the road itself. These are the mountain pass roads – the Passo del Gavia and Passo di Mortirolo, for

example and, most famously of all, the Passo dello Stelvio.

The Passo dello Stelvio, or Stelvio Pass, is a mountain pass in the eastern Alps, right on the border between Italy and Switzerland. It was built in the early nineteenth century as a way of linking the Austro-Hungarian Empire with Lombardy. Above it sits the *Dreisprachenspitze* – the 'Three Languages Peak', so called because this is the location where the influences of Italian, German and Romansch languages all cross. The pass itself is (technical term coming up) a whopper – eight miles long, a climb to 2,758 metres at its highest point. The road zig-zags its way up via 48 hairpins or *tornante*, and is the sort of road that cyclists and drivers dream about.

The Stelvio was first introduced into the Giro d'Italia in 1953. A legendary mountain needs a legendary winner and it was Fausto Coppi who reached the top first, on the way to his fifth and final Giro title. Not that his victory was without controversy: going into the stage, the *maglia rosa* (*see* Chapter Five) was on the shoulders of Hugo Koblet and the two riders had agreed an unwritten truce. Koblet would allow Coppi the stage win; Coppi wouldn't challenge Koblet for the race lead. On the stage itself, however, events played out differently. First Coppi pretended that he was struggling: then he sent the young Nino Defilippis to attack the small leading group. When Koblet tried (and failed) to bridge the gap, Coppi took off in a premeditated strop at his rival reneging on the deal. He ended up gaining four and half minutes over Koblet and the *maglia rosa* to boot.

DUTCH CORNER
Le Virage des Hollandais (Fr)

The Stelvio might have more *tornante*, but it is the *virages* of L'Alpe d'Huez that are arguably more famous. And of those 21 hairpin bends, it is the seventh – *Le Virage des Hollandais* that is perhaps the most famous of them all.

Just like the Passo dello Stelvio, L'Alpe d'Huez didn't make its Grand Tour debut until the early 1950s (1952 in this case). And just like the Stelvio, its greatness was sealed by Fausto Coppi being the first rider over the top. Since then, it has become one of the iconic stops on the Tour itinerary – to the point that it was climbed twice on the Tour's hundredth edition in 2013. It has been the sight of many famous battles over the years, with Hinault and LeMond riding up together in 1986 perhaps the most memorable of many memorable climbs.

It is the *virages* that give the mountain its amphitheatre feel, with claims that up to one million fans now line the climb each Tour (a long way from Coppi's victory, which was seen by barely a soul). The fans spill onto the road – creating a 'human corridor' as Richard Morre describes it in *Slaying The Badger*. He

quotes Andy Hampsten, who won the climb in 1992, saying, 'the sensation of passing through such a narrow opening in the crowd was the most beautiful and emotional thing I've ever experienced in my life.'

The 21 hairpins themselves are numbered rather than named, with the exception of one – corner seven – which has become known over the years as *Les Virage des Hollandais*: Dutch Corner. The Dutch affinity for L'Alpe d'Huez owes much to their early success on its slopes. After Coppi's initial victory, the mountain didn't host another finish until 1976. But between then and the end of the 1980s, Dutch riders won the climb eight times. Since then, the Dutch victories have dried up, but the fans remain.

Dutch Corner – which has a particularly good view looking back down the mountain – is where the Dutch fans congregate. It is a sea of orange; a wall of sound; a party that starts several days before the race and carries on long into the night. While other fans offer the riders some much needed water, the Dutch fans offer something stronger: in 2013, Lotto rider Adam Hansen helped himself to a beer as he went round the corner, a refreshment he repeated in 2015.

SUMMIT FINISH
Arrivée en Altitude (Fr)/Arrivo in Salita (It)

Fausto Coppi's victory on L'Alpe d'Huez in 1952 was not just the Tour's first visit to the mountain, it was also one of the first times that the Tour had ever had an *arrivée en altitude* – a summit finish. Indeed, in the early history of all the Grand Tours, such ends to a day's racing were far from common.

Money, no doubt, had a factor in this. Back in 1952, the Alpe d'Huez resort consisted of a single hotel. Now ski resorts can compete with the valley towns to pay good money for a stage finish: it makes financial sense for them to do so, bringing in the crowds to a resort that would otherwise be out of season. Today, the size of the *caravane* (*see* Chapter Eight) and cost of hosting a stage finish also rule out many iconic mountains previously used. The Puy-de-Dôme (roads too narrow) and Superbagnères (priced out) are among those no longer part of the pool of possible finishes.

Aside from money, an *arrivée en altitude* can have a decisive effect on the outcome of a race: 'a summit finish effectively divides the flock of valley sheep from the individual mountain goats', Geoffrey Nicholson once wrote. Certainly, the first summit finish of a race can often prove decisive to its outcome and tilts the overall rankings towards those who climb. As Nicholson commented on the battle for the 1976 *maillot jaune*, '[Maertens] climbed much better than Van Impe can sprint. But that's irrelevant. In a sprint you don't lose 4-51, even if you come last.'

Those designing a race have to decide how many summit finishes to include and, therefore, how climber-friendly/non-climber unfriendly the race will become as a result. The vogue at the Vuelta to up the number of summit finishes into double figures has not gone down well with the sprinters. Mark Cavendish makes the point that summit finishes are not always as interesting as the organizers like to think: rather than attacking and counter-attacking to break free, riders can end up in a sort of mountain time-trial mode, each climbing the slope at their own pace. The contrast between the two styles can be dramatic. At the 2014 Vuelta, Chris Froome kept to his own steady pace, ignoring the attacks off the front. He should have been dead and buried, but paced himself perfectly to the finish

CIMA COPPI (IT)

Named after Fausto Coppi, the *cima coppi* (literally the 'Coppi Summit') is the highest point of that year's Giro d'Italia and the first rider to reach it is rewarded accordingly. It was first awarded in 1965. In the Tour de France, the Souvenir Henri Desgrange (after the Tour's originator) is similarly awarded. In the Vuelta, the equivalent prize is the Cima Alberto Fernández, named after the 1980s Spanish cyclist of the same name. Fernández, known as *el Galleta* ('The biscuit') on account of the biscuit factories of his home town, finished third in the 1983 Vuelta, then second in the 1984 Vuelta, losing the race by just six seconds, still the smallest winning margin in Grand Tour history. Tragically, before he could attempt go one better and win the following race, he and his wife died in a car crash.

LA CUEÑA LES CABRES (SP)

At the end of the 1990s, the organizers of the Vuelta felt that they needed a mountain to match Ventoux, Tourmalet, Zoncolan and the other climbs that the Tour and the Giro had to offer. They came up with the Alto de l'Angliru – a former animal mountain track turned cyclist's nightmare. Among those sent to try it out before it was officially used was Pedro Delgado, who said, 'nothing like it has been seen before. Some will be putting their feet on the ground.'

The Angliru is not as long as some of the other iconic climbs, and might not be as high, but it more than makes up for this in terms of gradient. The steepest part of the Tourmalet is eleven per cent; the Stelvio twelve per cent; Alpe d'Huez thirteen per cent. The stiffest section of the Angliru has a whole half-dozen sections steeper than that. It's a climb that starts comparatively slowly, with the first half averaging about six per cent. But then it seriously kicks up. The second half doesn't dip below eleven per cent, with a number of sections well over that: Les Cabannes, 22 per cent; Lagos, 14.5 per cent; Les Picones, 20 per cent; Cobayos, 21.5 per cent; El Aviru, 21.5 per cent; and Les Piedrusines, 20 per cent. But the toughest of them all is La Cueña les Cabres at 23.5 per cent, just three miles from the summit.

The sharpness of the gradient and its position a few kilometres before the summit makes La Cueña les Cabres the perfect place to launch a race-changing attack. It was here that Alberto Contador took his chance in the 2008 Vuelta, breaking clear to take the race lead (from which he would go on to win his first Vuelta). It was also at this point, during the 2011 Vuelta, that race leader Bradley Wiggins ground to a halt, leaving teammate Chris Froome to chase after the Spaniard Juan José Cobo, who would go on to claim the red jersey and the overall victory (rescinded for doping in 2019). In 2013, it was the key point in the battle between Vincenzo Nibali and Chris Horner for the race lead: Nibali attacked three times but failed to dislodge Horner, who broke away shortly after to secure the red jersey and his first Grand Tour victory.

MUR (FL/FR)
Muro (It)

Mur or *Muro* means 'wall'. You can reasonably deduce that any hill with that at the start of its name is not going to be a bit of a pancake. Instead, you can expect something that might be short... but very, very steep.

Take the Mur de Huy, the climax of the Flèche Wallonne since 1983 and also a stage finish of the Tour de France in 2015. The kicker here is the S-bend about half way up, which hits 25 per cent: if you're not at the front and the sort of rider who packs an explosive punch, you can forget about winning. Or take the Muro di Guardiagrele in Italy, as featured in the 2014 Tirreno–Adriatico – average gradient 22 per cent; steepest section, 30 per cent. 'If I said that was fun, that'd be a lie,' Marcel Kittel said afterwards.

Then there's the Muro di Sormano, introduced to the Giro di Lombardia in 1960. With an average gradient of 15 per cent and a steepest section of 25 per cent, it fulfilled one newspaper's prediction that 'we will all be watching the national pushing festival.' Many riders ended up either walking up or having their fans on the slope to give them a push. After rider complaints, the 'Wall' was dropped, only returning to the course 50 years later.

FALSE FLAT
Faux Plat (Fr)

A bit of road that looks flat but isn't. A false flat can be deceptive in two ways. Firstly, it can appear flat whilst actually having a small gradient of one or two per cent, leaving the cyclist wondering why they're finding the route so hard. In *The Great Bike Rice*, Geoffrey Nicholson describes the section between Col du Luitel and L'Alpe d'Huez as '20 kilometres of *faux plat*, a road that looks flat but is imperceptibly rising towards the base of Alpe d'Huez.'

Secondly, a false flat can be found on a mountainside: a shallower section after a steep gradient that can feel flat by comparison, but turns out to be anything but. The Amstel Gold race climaxes on the Cauberg – a short but deadly 1.5-kilometre climb, that goes from two to six to nine to eleven per cent. As the gradient drops, the unsuspecting rider thinks they've made it, but the last 500 metres is all false flat, an energy-sapping finish that does for anyone who has nothing left to give.

LACETS (FR)

Lacets is French for shoelaces and neatly sums up the stunning new addition to the Tour's mountain schedule in the 2015 edition. The Lacets de Montvernier is not a long Alpine climb at 3.4 kilometres. Nor is it overly steep, with an average gradient of 8.4 per cent – on the Tour's grading, it only ranked as a Category 2 climb. Yet what the Lacets had going for it was those shoelaces. Eighteen hairpin bends, just three less than L'Alpe d'Huez, yet packed into a far shorter space. The narrow road twists every 150 metres and neither the *caravane* (*see* Chapter 8) nor or even spectators were allowed on the climb.

All of which didn't seem very Tour de France. Which seemed a Good Thing – that the organizers were happy to try something new. As it turned out, the race's first visit to the climb looked great, but the way the stage played out lacked excitement: such were the twists, it was difficult to attack. But the potential for drama remains – in another year, this climb could offer up a pivotal moment.

VENTOUX
Le Mont Chauve (Fr)/*Le Géant de Provence* (Fr)

The Bald Mountain. The Giant of Provence. Ventoux. First climbed competitively in the Tour de France, first used as a stage finish in 1958, Ventoux is a mountain unlike any other in the Tour de France, lacking the particular characteristics of the climbs in the Alps and the Pyrenees. Instead, it offers riders a steady, relentless ride up to the summit, out and above the tree line into a barren, rocky landscape that commentators and journalists try and fail to resist describing as lunar.

Sometimes it is the mountain's oppressive heat that is the enemy. It helped to do for Tom Simpson in 1967, though he certainly wasn't the first to suffer – Ferdi Kübler, for example, struggled with heatstroke in 1955. At other times, it can be the wind in this exposed and barren landscape that can be a rider's nemesis.

Ventoux is a mountain laden with history and prestige. Tom Simpson's memorial, on the way to the summit, is a reminder of Tours past and the sacrifices made by riders in the hope of victory. The Tour planners have used it sparingly as a summit, which serves to maintain some of its aura: the 2021 double ascent will only be the eleventh year that the Tour has visited the mountain since 1958 – a third as many as L'Alpe d'Huez. It means that for both fans and riders alike, a Tour visit there is always something special.

TWELVE | Tactics

There's more than one way to win a bike race. Ever since Henri Desgrange, the Tour's originator, lost his battle to prevent cycling from becoming a team event, the sport has developed a rich vein of tactics and strategies that don't always make sense to the naked eye. The rider who wins a race isn't always the best rider there, but the one who has played his particular cards to pedaling perfection.

WHEEL-SUCKER
Succeur de Roues (Fr)/ Succhia Ruota (It)
'Nobody likes a wheel-sucker,' states Rule #67 of *The Rules*,. 'Do your time in the wind.' 'Riding wheels and jumping past at the end is one thing and one thing only: poor sportsmanship.'

But is that the same in road racing, or is it smart tactics? At the 2012 Milan–San Remo, Vincenzo Nibali broke clear on the Poggio climb as the race neared its conclusion. Fabian Cancellara went after him and as he made the move across, the Australian rider Simon Gerrans went with him. Gerrans sat on Cancellara's wheel all the way to the finish, where he broke clear with the line in sight to win the race. A few months later at the 2012 Tour de France, an almost identical scenario played out. On the first stage from Liège to Seraing, it was Sylvain Chavanel who attacked on the final Category 4 climb: Cancellara followed, taking Peter Sagan with him. Sagan stayed behind until the end of the race, when he moved round to sprint to victory.

So much of road racing is about saving energy: the man in front is protecting the man behind from the wind. So in these two examples, Cancellera did the lion's share of the work and Sagan and Gerrans got the wins. Is that unfair on Cancellara? Yes and no. If a time-trial is a 'race of truth', with the strongest rider winning, then a normal stage is a race of tactics, with the smarter man taking the victory. Having broken clear, it is down to the escapee to lose the rider behind. The only incentive for the person on his wheel to do a turn at the front is if he thinks help is needed to ensure the breakaway stays away.

After Sagan's victory in the Tour stage, Cancellara said, 'Once I made my attack it would have been good to get some help. In Milan–San Remo it was the same but I'm not going to attack and ease off and end up somewhere out the back – that is not my style: when I go, then I go and really put the hammer down until the end.' A different rider might have called Sagan's bluff, slowing down to allow the possibility of the bunch catching up if he doesn't help. But with Cancellera telegraphing his probable tactics, Sagan knew that was going to be unlikely.

Over the course of a race, there can be riders not doing their turn for all sorts of reasons. In a breakaway, a rider might sit on the back if their team is leading the GC and they've been sent up to keep watch on proceedings. As much as the other riders might do that elbow-waving manouevre to say, 'your turn', they can sit there with an apologetic 'only following orders' shrug. Sometimes there may be more incentive for certain riders to work than others.

Perhaps the most famous perceived wheelsucker was Joop Zoetemelk, who finished second in the Tour six times in the 1970s and early 1980s (as well as winning it in 1980). Those early second places came behind Eddy Merckx and there is a well-worked cycling joke about how Zoetemelk was the only rider never to tan on account of spending the entire race in Merckx's shadow. To be fair to Zoetemelk, he may just have been riding in the shadow of Merckx's greatness – less wheelsucking and more the only rider able to stay on his wheel. Fairly or not, the nicknames The Wheelsucker and The Rat proved hard to shift, despite his Tour, Vuelta and World Road Race wins.

PIANO (IT)

That's *piano*, as in Italian for 'quiet'. Back in the day, the Giro and other races would often be ridden *piano* for much of a flat stage. Local riders would be allowed to go off ahead to say hello to friends and family and everyone would

take it easy, as the Eagles (*not* of Toledo) once put it. Only towards the end of the stage would riders begin to go through the gears to ramp up speed before the finish.

(HARD) TEMPO

Tempo riding is all about setting a pace and sticking to it. It makes for a smooth ride – as if the peloton are part of one smooth multi-team time-trial, with one or two dominant outfits setting the tone. It means that they can set the peloton pace at a speed that their team leader is comfortable with.

It is a tactic that has been used successfully by the likes of Team Sky in recent years. Once the race jersey is in their possession, then the best way to fend off attacks from rivals is to sit on the front of the group and set the pace so high that no-one has the energy left to attack. One by one, the *domestiques* (*see* Chapter Three) will do their shift at the front, keeping the speed up until they are so spent that they have to peel off. If the tactic works, then the race lead remains secure. If it doesn't, then the race leader can reach the business end of a race with no riders left for support.

The other problem with this tactic is an aesthetic one. Keeping the pace high to stop any attacks might bring in the victories, but it can be dull as anything to watch.

TIME-TRIAL MODE

Once the team have been riding high tempo (*see* above) for most of a stage, it is left to the team leaders to do their stuff on the slopes of the decisive mountains. For those riders who are 'all-rounders' rather than natural climbers, this is usually a moment to minimize losses and resist the urge to follow the more attacking style of the other riders in the race. This was certainly the case for the likes of Chris Froome and Tom Dumolin in the 2014 and 2015 Vueltas. Their preference was for a sustained, steady, even tempo up the mountainside – allowing a Contador or a Valverde or an Aru to hare off ahead. They hoped their tortoise-like time-trialling response would ultimately reel in the climbers, or if not, keep them in touching distance so that they could take back the time in the time-trials. Such tactics can be deceptive to watch: it can look like a rider is struggling when in fact they are riding within themselves. But in the same way that high-tempo riding can bring in results but make for poor viewing, winning races in time-trial mode can lack the sparkle and romance that the sport can provide.

SCATTISTA (IT)

Scattista is an Italian word used to describe a rider who is known for their quick bursts of speed. In contrast to a rider who takes a mountain climb at a steady pace, a *scalatore* (*see grimpeur* Chapter Three) who is also a *scattista* will be looking to use their combined skills at climbing and acceleration to drop their rivals and build up a big enough gap to take them to the finish. It's a more stop-start way of racing than the high-tempo approach and though in terms of energy conservation it might not always be the most practical, it makes for more dramatic and exciting racing – as in recent Vueltas where the likes of Valverde, Rodriquez and Contador have knocked the cycling equivalent of seven bells out of each other.

Classic riders in this style are Marco Pantani and Charly Gaul. The speed with which Pantani put distance between himself and Jan Ullrich on the slopes of the Galibier during the 1998 Tour was staggering. Similarly, in the 1950s, Charly Gaul – nicknamed The Angel of the Mountains – had the ability to fly away from his rivals.

BLOCKING

A spoiling tactic. The tempo of the peloton is dictated by the person at the front, so if a team wants the peloton to slow down – perhaps to stop them catching up with a breakaway – a supposedly helpful turn at the front can turn out to be a hindrance if the rider is going slow. It's a bit of a fine art – go too slow and everyone will know what you're up to and shout at you to get out of the way.

There's also the question of blocking in terms of a sprint finish. As the lead-out men peel off, they should get out of the way to let the others racing for the line get through. While there are rules and regulations about getting into someone else's racing line, there may be times to take one for the team: it's the lead-out man, rather than the sprinter who will be penalized for such actions, in the same way that a footballer might take a yellow card to stop the opposing team getting up the pitch. As with slowing the peloton down, there's an art to doing this without getting caught.

COUP DE CHACAL (FR)

The 'jackal's trick'. This is a surprise attack just before the end of a race, usually with a couple of kilometres to go, as the peloton and lead-out trains are gearing up for a sprint finish. It's a tactic suited to a rider who knows that they wouldn't win in a sprint and that their best chance of success is to get out in front and bury themselves in the hope of staying there. The terms comes from the behaviour of the creature itself: as the *Doppio* blog puts it, 'a piece of opportunistic scavenging befitting the carnivorous creature from which it takes its name.' In recent years, the tactic has also become known as a *Coup de Cancellera*, given the rider's predilection for such a move.

POSITIONING

In many races, the art of positioning can be crucial in deciding the outcome of the race. A good rider will have studied the roadbook carefully and know the pinch points ahead – the moments when staying towards the front will be absolutely crucial.

That is certainly the case in Classics such as Paris–Roubaix and the Strade Bianche. If you're not in a good position when these races hit the cobbles or gravel, then such is the tightness and difficulty of the terrain that you're left hoping that you're not going to get stuck behind a crash or inexperienced riders. It's also true in the opening stages of a Grand Tour when pile-ups can be par for the course. One of the crucial stages of the 2015 Tour was stage 2 along the Zeeland coast: Froome and Contador were paying attention; Quintana and Nibali weren't, caught out by a combination of wind and crashes. Quintana ended up losing a minute and a half to Froome – about the same time he later gained over him on the climb of Alpe d'Huez. As Daniel Friebe wryly tweeted, 'Chris Froome, the first man to win the Tour de France in Holland.'

Positioning in a sprint is crucial, too. Mark Cavendish described the thought process to Lionel Birnie in an article for *The Cycling Anthology*: 'I know if I go from this position to that position, there's going to be a space opening up there, so I can go there, but that means that this person will move up there so I could be boxed in... there's a space on the right but a team could come up that side, so I'd rather be on the left where there isn't room for them to come up on that side... ' A great sprinter like Cavendish can sniff out the openings, knowing instinctively the right line to take and also the wrong one that could leave him going down the sprinting equivalent of a cul-de-sac.

BONKING /BLOWING UP
Fringale (Fr)/ Défaillance (Fr) /*Crisi di fame* (It)

Sustenance is crucial for a bike rider – keeping the energy coming in through food and drink to balance the energy going out through pedalling away up mountain after mountain. Get that balance wrong and blood sugar levels can drop. Once you go in cycling, you really go: the effects of what the French call *fringale*, the Italians a *crisi di fame* and the English bonking, can be dramatic, with riders losing serious amounts of time as they wobble across the road. It's the reason that Chris Froome risked a penalty by taking an illegal gel on the slopes of Alpe d'Huez during his 2013 Tour de France victory. 'It was horrible, not having the energy,' he wrote in *The Climb*. 'Whoa. Focus. My head was all over the place. There was less and less power in my legs, just jelly. I had nothing.' Froome had Richie Porte to thank for getting him to the finish – the 20-second penalty he got was nothing compared to the minutes he'd have lost without that gel.

Eddy Merckx experienced a similar situation on his epic stage win in the Pyrenees during the 1969 Tour. Out in front but with 56 kilometres to go, he bonked and over the next sixteen kilometres lost two minutes to the chasing riders. As William Fotheringham writes in his biography of Merckx, 'suddenly, his strength ran out. His style was no longer smooth. He was sweating heavily. He did not panic, however, merely steadying his pace so that he could eat, before going on.'

A BAD DAY
Giornata no (It)/*Un Jour Sans* (Fr)

A 'no day' in Italian. A 'day without' in French. A bad day at the cycling office in whatever language you ride, this describes those times when you turn the pedals and find nothing there in the legs.

Such a day is synonymous with Jan Ullrich's disastrous defence of his yellow

jersey during the 1998 Tour. Yes, Marco Pantani took off like a bullet up the slopes of the Galibier, but the eventual time gap between the two of them – eight minutes – was part Pantani brilliance and part Ullrich just having an absolute shocker.

DANCING ON THE PEDALS

Different riders bring with them different pedaling styles. Some are more attractive to look at than others. Chris Froome, for example, is all about high cadence – staying in the saddle and turning the pedals round like a hamster on a wheel; all the time with his elbows and head down. A successful, if ungainly, style of riding but one that suits his frame.

Riders with other builds pedal differently. I don't know if the TV commentator Phil Liggett invented the phrase 'dancing on the pedals', but his poetic use of it aptly describes the technique of riders such as Alberto Contador. He is a rider who is up and out of the saddle on the climbs; turning his pedals gracefully, looking up rather than down. It's not for everyone, but for those riders who master it, it's a smooth, skilful way of riding your bike.

THE TRAIN

It's the end of a long day's stage. The breakaways have been reeled in. The peloton is all together. The *flamme rouge* (*see* Chapter Six) is approaching. It's time for the bunch sprint – that shoot-out of the fastest men on two wheels. And as the various designated sprinters are gearing up to duke it out, hitting the front with a few hundred metres to go, it is down to the hard work of their teammates to get them there – a carefully practiced lead-out line known as the train.

Mark Cavendish's golden stage-winning streak between 2009 and 2011 was in part down to the well-oiled tactics of his HTC Colombia team. Every member of that team had their part to play in setting up the sprint. The process would start early on, with *domestiques* (*see* Chapter Three) such as Lars Bak or Danny Pate sitting on the front of the peloton at a high pace, discouraging any attacks and attempting to keep the peloton together. Cavendish, intermediate sprints apart, would spend the majority of the day safely ensconced in the peloton, saving his energy.

The HTC train would shift into gear with about 10 kilometres to go. Moving to the front of the bunch, they'd ride in a single line like a team time-trial, with each member (Cav excepted) pulling a big turn on the front. With the pace heading towards 60 kilometres per hour, the final few kilometres would see Tony Martin doing a turn from about three kilometres, Matt Goss with about

1.5 kilometres to go, and Bernard Eisel, the *captaine de route*, moving to the front under the *flamme rouge*. Mark Renshaw, the lead-out man *par excellence*, would then bury himself at speeds of up to 70 kilometres per hour, before the 'Manx Missile' would be unleashed with 200-300 metres to go. His kick of speed – up to 1500 watts of power – would hopefully take him over the finish line in victory pose.

The development of the train in sprint finishes is a relatively new phenomenon in cycling. In the 1960s, Rik Van Looy's Flandria team would form what became known as the Red Guard (because of the colour their shirts). Rather than a single-line train, they'd mass across the front of the group to deter and chase down any attacks, keeping things together for Van Looy (and later Freddy Maertens) for the sprint to the finish. After that, sprints became something of a pushing-and-pulling free-for-all until the arrival of Jean-Paul van Poppel's Superconfex team in their lime-green shirts. Van Poppel (who won six stages in the 1987 and 1988 Tours de Frances, and the green jersey in the former), was helped enormously by his team, who attempted to control the race from about five kilometres to go. In the 1990s, the main express service was the 'Red Train' of Saeco, who steered the Italian sprinter Marco Cipollini to many of his 42 Giro stage wins, as well as twelve Tour de France and three Vuelta victories (Cipollini would have won many more of the latter two, were it not for his annual dismount at the sight of the first mountain pass).

The HTC train in the late noughties set the bar higher again. It was perhaps no coincidence that Cavendish struggled when he switched to Team Sky (taking only Eisel of his original train with him) and returned to form when he was reunited with Mark Renshaw at Etixx-Quick-Step. Today, the sprint train has evolved again. Rather than just one train guiding the peloton in the finishing stage, the final kilometres of a race often feature two or three trains vying at the front for control – a bit like rival Victorian railway companies, each going full-steam ahead on competing lines to the same destination.

LA COURSE EN TÊTE (FR)

La Course en Tête is a style of racing associated with Eddy Merckx. Rather than riding conservatively, marking your rivals and conserving your energy for the set-piece stages such as the time-trials or mountain top finishes and then defending your lead once ahead, *la course en tête* involves taking the fight to your opponents.

As William Fotheringham explains in his biography of Merckx, the tactic 'is centred on the premise that as much physical and mental energy is used in chasing down moves as is spent in making them.' Therefore, rather than sitting back, you're better off attacking yourself – making your presence felt at the front of the peloton and grinding down your rivals with a constant barrage of moves. Such a strategy means that you have to be up there, rather than cossetted within the team, or having a break in the centre of the bunch. It means being opportunist – taking your chances whenever they come and never allowing your opponents to switch off.

As tactics go, it obviously helps if you're Eddy Merckx. But it's an offensive strategy that other riders do use, just not with the frequency of Merckx. In the 2014 Tour, Vincenzo Nibali could have been described as riding *en tête*: even before the mountains had been reached, he had taken valuable time on stage 2 in Sheffield and over the cobbles on stage 5 to Arenberg. And even once he was comfortably in yellow, he attacked again on stage 18 up the Hautacam, putting further daylight between him and his competitors. Nibali, like Merckx in his heyday, was totally dominating the race, whatever the *parcours*.

MARGINAL GAINS

'We're good at timed events, good at the physiological stuff, but it gets patchy when tactics are involved,' Dave Brailsford said '...This is a technical sport, there is a lot of other... stuff. Bikes, wheels, helmets, clothing, all that stuff. Is there anything we can do to improve that?'

In his autobiography *Triumphs and Turbulence,* Chris Boardman suggests that the start of the Marginal Gains philosophy can be traced back to the above conversation with Dave Brailsford in a coffee shop at Manchester Piccadilly Station in summer 2004. At the time, Brailsford and Boardman were both working for British Cycling, with Boardman on, well, board, as a Technical Advisor. Following the conversation, Boardman and a small group of colleagues, who became known as the Secret Squirrel Club (*see also Il Scoiattolo de Navigli*, Chapter Ten), set about pulling apart received wisdom on cycling in the laboratory and wind tunnel, to see if anything could be done differently. The theory was that instead of doing one thing 100 per cent better, you could do 100 things one per cent better, to create the same improvement in performance.

It is a philosophy that took Boardman and the researchers to some strange places: making Rob Hayles cycle naked in a wind tunnel so that they could compare his times against those with clothing ('Rob asked if all the flopping about would adversely affect his aero performance. Sandy, who was running the test, told him that he doubted the wind tunnel instruments were sensitive enough to pick it up'). On another occasion, there was a lengthy conversation about breaking Ed Clancy's collarbone and resetting his shoulders to make him more aerodynamic. But in the end, they just went for making cycling suits out of different fabrics. For the cyclists involved, the demands were as great as the rewards: after Victoria Pendleton cycled her last event at the 2012 Olympics, she expressed her huge relief at never again having to spend hours refining her position in wind tunnels or squeezing into a 'skin suit'.

Just as marginal gains delivered for British Cycling at the London Olympics, so Dave Brailsford and his team have taken on the approach with similar attention to detail at Team Sky. To ensure a good night's sleep and help recovery, for example, the team ensure every rider has their own hypoallergenic mattress, duvet and pillow, rather than risking a night of dodgy springs and bed bugs. It's an approach that remains restless and doesn't always succeed: a plan for riders to sleep in motorhomes in 2015 didn't come off after Tour de France officials ruled that the designated hotels had to be used. But where it has worked, results have been spectacular. The original five-year plan was to win the Tour within five years from a standing start. They did it twice.

THIRTEEN | Cheating

'Competition produces doping,' Paul Fornel wrote in *Vélo*, 'just as taxes produce fraud.' With the extraordinary asks that race organizers have made on riders over the century, there is perhaps an inevitability that some riders have chosen to go to, well, extraordinary lengths, to stay one bike's length ahead of the field. Those of a nervous disposition, or who like their cycling romance untainted, should look away now.

LITTLE BLACK BOTTLE

As long as there have been cycling races, there have been riders taking drugs. Way back in the 1890s, one of the leading British trainers was James 'Choppy' Warburton, whose riders included Arthur Linton (who won the 1896 Bordeaux–Paris) and Jimmy Michael (who won the world title in 1895). Linton, the last British rider to win a Classic until Tom Simpson in the 1960s, did not win the race without controversy.

Firstly, on the run in to Paris, he veered off the main course to go over the wrong bridge over the Seine, leading to calls from the second and third place riders for him to be disqualified. It transpired that Linton had used the original planned route, but because the bridge was being repaired the route had been altered – as Linton didn't read the French newspapers where the announcement was made, he was unaware.

On the way towards Paris, however, a different sort of controversy had also unfolded. By the time the race reached Orléans, the French rider Gaston

Rivière was not only comfortably ahead of Linton, but the British rider looked something of a spent force. 'I saw him at Tours,' a journalist for *Cyclers News* reported, 'when he came in with glassy eyes and tottering limbs, and in a high state of nervous excitement. I then heard him swear, a very rare occurrence with him, but after a rest he was off again, though none of us expected he would go very far. At Orléans at five o'clock in the morning Choppy and I looked after a wreck.'

This wreck, though, turned things around to first catch and then overhaul Rivière for the race win. How did he do this? The answer may or may not be found in Choppy's 'Little Black Bottle', which the trainer ostentatiously gave to his riders to give them a boost. What was actually in Choppy's bottle is one of cycling's mysteries: 'magic', claimed the trainer himself. Others have suggested that heroin or a concoction including ingredients such as caffeine, ether, cocaine and strychnine seems rather more likely. In the USA at the time, riders were drinking such a combination, which was known as 'American Coffee' (and you thought drinking Chai Latte was bad for you). All were available at the chemist and not banned in terms of cycling – doping tests were at this point still many decades away from being introduced.

The mystery of Choppy's black bottle deepened further the following year. At a race in South London in 1896, Jimmy Michael took a sip from Choppy's black bottle, only to start cycling in the wrong direction as a result. Accusations poured in from all sides: Michael claimed Choppy was trying to poison him because he was trying to extract himself from a contract with the trainer; others suggested that Michael was making it up in order to give him a reason to leave Choppy. Whatever the truth, Choppy was banned by the National Cyclist's Union. He died the following year, still trying to clear his name.

DYNAMITE

'You have no idea what the Tour de France is. It's a cavalry. We suffer on the road. But do you want to see how we keep going?'

In 1924, Henri Pélissier and his brother Francis were two of the riders interviewed by *Le Petit Parisien* journalist Albert Londres for what became one of the most famous pieces of cycling writing: '*Les Forcats de la Route*', or 'Convicts of the Road'. Pélissier, who had won the Tour de France the previous year, was never shy in giving his opinions on what Henri Desgrange, the first organizer of the Tour, had inflicted on the riders. And in Albert Londres, he found a willing audience. Comparing the race to hard labour, the Pélissier brothers went on to empty their pockets to reveal how the riders made it through. There was cocaine 'for the eyes', chloroform 'for the gums', horse ointment for the knees and 'pills. Do you want to see the pills?' Henri Pélissier asked, the riders showing Londres their boxes. His brother Francis summed it up: 'we run on dynamite.'

It's not known if the Pélissier brothers literally ran on dynamite, but if they had taken nitroglycerine, they wouldn't have been the first riders to have done so – it was taken by early riders to help with breathing. And you thought hiding urine up your anus was a crazy thing to do (*see* below).

AMPHETAMINES
La Bomba (It)

By the 1950s, the cycling drug of choice was amphetamines. One user was Fausto Coppi, who was quite upfront about taking them. Asked by Mario Ferretti in an interview after the end of his career whether he doped, Coppi's response was clear: 'Yes, and those who say otherwise aren't worth talking to about cycling.' Asked when he used amphetamines, Coppi's response was 'when necessary' and when asked when necessary, his response was 'almost always'.

Coppi's openness about his use was no different to the Pélissier brothers a quarter of a century earlier. Cycling races were hard, the argument went; this is what riders did to get through them. Indeed, it was apparently such a given that by the early 1930s, the official Tour regulations reminded riders that they would have to pay for 'stimulants, tonics and doping'.

Different riders had their own predilections. Alfredo Binda believed that raw eggs gave him a boost: he ate 34 to get him going before winning the 1926 Tour of Lombardy. Gino Bartali, meanwhile, was more of an espresso man: he'd down 28 in a day. Coppi, too, liked his coffee, but that wasn't enough on its own. His preference was for a concoction called *la bomba* – defined by William Fotheringham in *Fallen Angel* as, 'seven or eight espresso coffees, sugar, peptocola and two or three mild amphetamine pills.'

Amphetamines didn't give the riders any physiological advantage. Instead, their effect was more on the mind: pepping the rider up, numbing the pain, keeping them going. Originally, the drug came into usage during the Second World War, when the US Airforce gave it to pilots to combat fatigue. And while there are obviously benefits for an endurance race, they come at a cost. Because the body gets used to amphetamines, you have to take increasing amounts to get the same response. And by helping the rider to ignore any pain they might be experiencing, they may override any warning signs that their body is giving them – one of the factors behind the death of Tom Simpson on Ventoux in 1967.

BAD FISH

Stage 14 of the 1962 Tour de France, and the Wiel's-Groene Leeuw team asked the race organizers to delay the start by ten minutes because their team leader, Hans Junkermann, lying eighth overall, was feeling unwell. In fact, Junkermann was feeling terrible, having been up most of the night. And although that day's start was put back, it did him little good – he was soon off the back and ended up having to abandon.

Junkermann's reasoning for feeling unwell was simple. 'Bad fish', he explained. He'd had it for supper and hadn't been right ever since. Pretty soon, it transpired that Junkermann wasn't the only to have suffered from this unfortunate fish supper: Willy Schroeder, Gastone Nencini and Karl-Heinz Kunde were among the eleven riders who had to withdraw from the race.

And yet two small niggly details left this mass abandon feeling a little, well, fishy. Firstly, it only seemed to be the riders who'd got this extreme bout of food poisoning and none of the support staff also staying at the hotels. And secondly, the hotels who'd hosted the riders and were keen not to suffer negative publicity from having poisoned so many guests, showed the press the menu from the previous night: the only way the fish was off, was in terms of it being off the menu completely.

At the Woodstock Music Festival in 1969, a warning was read out on-stage for festival-goers to watch out for some brown acid circulating, which was 'bad' and liable to give you freaky hallucinations. Quite what Jenkermann and the other 1962 Tour riders had taken was never proven, though both race organizer Jacques Goddet and race doctor Pierre Dumas had their suspicions that had been the riders had suffered from a similarly dodgy batch of whatever performance-enhancing drug they had been given.

The 'Bad Fish' episode wasn't the last time that food and drugs got mixed up at the Tour de France. At the 2010 Tour, Alberto Contador's steak supper, brought over from Spain by a friend, turned out to be contaminated with traces of clenbuterol. Like the 1962 hoteliers, the Spanish meat industry were quick to weigh in, describing the claims as 'a gratuitous attack on Spanish beef producers without any basis.' Contador was subsequently stripped of his Tour title.

THE ANQUETIL COCKTAIL

If Fausto Coppi was direct when it came to talking about drug use, then Jacques Anquetil was outspoken. 'If you want to accuse me of having doped, it's not difficult,' he once said. 'All you have to do is look at my thighs and buttocks – they're veritable pin cushions. You have to be an imbecile or a hypocrite to imagine that a professional cyclist who races 235 days a year in all weathers can keep going without stimulants.' It was Anquetil who led the rider's protests when drug testing came in and on occasions, he simply refused to participate. When he broke The Hour record in 1967, he declined to give a urine sample afterwards, and the record was never officially ratified.

Pierre Dumas, the race doctor at the Tour de France in the 1960s coined the phrase the 'Anquetil Cocktail' to describe the drug use of the time. This 'cocktail' consisted of three elements. The first of these was a painkiller, such as morphine or palfium. These dealt with muscle pain, but slowed things down. Hence cocktail ingredient number two – the stimulant – usually in the form of amphetamines. However, the problem with amphetamines is that they might keep you alert during the race, but also well into the night afterwards. When Coppi beat Koblet on the Stelvio Pass in 1953, his *gregario* (*see domestique*, Chapter Three) Ettore Milano was despatched before the stage to check Koblet's eyes, to work out if he'd been up all night from the effects of amphetamines the day before. He had. So the third component in the Anquetil Cocktail are sleeping pills. And then the next day, if you'll forgive the pun, the whole cycle can start all over again...

HIDEY HOLE

July 1978 and the Belgian rider Michel Pollentier wins the stage up L'Alpe d'Huez to take the *maillot jaune* (*see* Chapter Five) ahead of Joop Zoetemelk and Bernard Hinault. His friend and teammate Freddy Maertens has a bottle of chilled champagne waiting for him back at the hotel. Could a rider's life get any better? All that stood between Pollentier and a night of celebration was the formality of the trip to the doping control caravan.

Such was the shift that Pollentier had pulled on the way up Alpe d'Huez that, as Peter Cossins describes in *Alpe d'Huez*, 'he had been unable to control his bladder and had peed in his shorts and all over his bike.' Unfortunate stuff – it meant he'd have to go and get a change of clothing before the drugs test. Back to the hotel he went, returning to the control caravan just within the hour limit.

Since drugs tests had been introduced to the Tour in the late 1960s, some riders had gone to ever more extreme lengths to fool the system. The trick involved supplying the testers with a sample not of your own urine, which might prove positive, but someone else's. How might one pull off such an act? With a condom full of clean urine, secreted under the armpit, a tube running down the back and round, then sellotaped to the penis. One quick squeeze of the condom under the arm, and voilà! One negative test and you were away.

The ruse only worked, however, if the testers allowed the riders to keep their clothes on. Technically, they should strip to allow the tester to see the sample being delivered. In reality, testers often let the riders keep their clothes on and just turn their back. That was what Pollentier was anticipating. Unfortunately for him, the official wanted to do things properly and discovered his armpit-piss contraption. Pollentier was disqualified and suspended for two months.

There was another place that Pollentier could have hidden the condom. Peter Cossins mentions the claims of Freddy Maertens that the urine was actually hidden in Pollentier's anus. Whether that is the case or not, it was a regular practice to use what was known as the 'hidey hole', as described in *Breaking The Chains* by Willy Voets, in the chapter helpfully titled 'Tube Up The Bum.' Voets describes the procedure thus: 'in the team car, when the rider comes to change before going to the drug control… you slip the part of the tube fitted with the condom up the backside, inject clean urine up the tube with a large syringe, cork it and stick it to the skin following the line of the perineum, as far as the testicles.'

Voets' top tip is to cover the tube with hair – 'carpet pile or any short hair' to disguise the tube should the tester come looking. The advantage over the armpit method is that because the urine is hidden in the anus, it is kept warm, rather than being suspiciously armpit-cold. Voets warns that the technique is 'not for the faint-hearted. You can't be too squeamish if you're going to walk towards a doctor in charge of the dope test with something like that up your backside.'

EDGAR ALLEN POE

Juice. OJ. Salsa. Vitamin E. Therapy. Altitude Training in a Syringe. Edgar Allen Poe. Erythropoietin. EPO. By the end of the early 1980s and the start of the 1990s, the drugs game in cycling had changed. Amphetamine use almost seemed quaint (though Paul Kimmage in his book *Rough Ride* cites them as still being used in smaller races in the mid-1980s). Doping had moved on to steroids for strength and cortisone for reducing pain and increasing airflow.

But EPO offered riders a way of increasing the number of red blood cells produced, which increases the supply of oxygen to the muscles. Or as Tony Rominger explained to David Millar in *Racing In The Dark,* 'EPO allows you to go faster for longer.' How much faster and for how much longer? A laboratory study by the *European Journal of Applied Physiology* in 2007 tested a group of 16 cyclists over a 13-week period. In tests on peak power output and a trial to exhaustion, the cyclists on EPO had an improvement in peak power output by thirteen per cent and extended their time to exhaustion by 54 per cent. That's just a small sample, but gives an indication of the large improvements that EPO can bring.

The other great thing about EPO for cyclists wanting to use it, was that there was no test for it. Because red blood cells are naturally produced, it was impossible to detect which riders were using EPO – even if their speeds and performances were making it clear that something was going on. It turned a good rider such as Bjarne Riis into a Tour-winning one: Riis won the Tour in 1996 and in 2007 admitted that he used EPO for a sustained period between 1993 and 1998. He describes his panic over the police raids following the Festina revelations at the 1998 Tour, and flushing his drugs down the toilet after a tip-off that the police were on their way: he didn't use the drug again.

Without a test for EPO throughout the 1990s, the only way that the authorities could keep tabs on riders using the drug was by monitoring their hematocrit levels. Anything above 50 per cent was considered suspicious and a rider registering over that level was suspended for a fortnight. It wasn't an exact system and some riders with naturally high levels of red blood cells suffered, but for riders and their trainers, the challenge was to get their hematocrit level as close to 50 as possible. Riis's nickname in the peloton was Mr 60 per cent, based on rumours of his hematocrit scores; Jeff D'Hondt, *soigneur* (*see* Chapter Eight) for T-Mobile at the time, claims (though Riis denies it) that he even registered 64 per cent at one point.

Tests for EPO since 2000 have led to cyclists beating the system by other methods (*see* below); but while its use has declined at the top level of the sport, a 2015 *Guardian* report suggested that it was still common in lower-level cycling events and had even spread to the amateur level, resulting in events with 'middle-aged businessmen winning on EPO.' In 2015, the advent of the FG-4592 drug offered the prospect of EPO in pill form. Although the drug was still being tested and wasn't considered suitable for human consumption, there were already cases of riders testing positive for it.

OIL CHANGE
A Cambiar El Aceite (Sp)
Once a test for EPO appeared at the turn of the new millennium, dopers needed another way to beat the authorities. The result was a return to blood doping. Originally used in the late 1970s and early 1980s before the practice was banned, the process involves taking a unit of blood out of the body, whizzing it through a centrifuge to increase the all-important number of red blood cells and then returning the blood to the body at the required moment. As a process, it offered a more powerful kick than EPO. In Tyler Hamilton's *The Secret Race*, he suggests that a transfusion of treated blood immediately boosts a rider's hematocrit level by about three points, which 'correlated to a

three per cent increase in power.' EPO, by contrast, offers a more gradual rise. And like EPO in the early 1990s, blood transfusions were sold to riders as 'undetectable, 100 percent safe – if you did them properly.'

In *The Secret Race*, Hamilton describes the first time he did an 'oil change' in 2000, as the process is known in Spain. Travelling down to a village in the south of Spain, he 'expected to see a sophisticated medical setup, but this looked more like a junior-high science experiment.' In went a needle, 'about the size and shape of a coffee stirrer,' and then Hamilton found himself 'watching a big clear plastic bag slowly filling up with [his own] dark red blood. You never forget it.' A few weeks later during the Tour de France, the blood went back in: it felt cold, because it had been kept in the cooler. But once the transfusion was over, the effect was immediate. 'At dinner, I notice a strange sensation: I felt good. Normally at this point in the Tour, you feel a bit like a zombie – tired, shuffling, staring. Now, however, I felt springy, healthy. Euphoric, even, as if I'd had a couple cups of really good coffee.'

The trick with using blood bags is timing. Blood cells can only survive out of the body for about a month. On top of which, you can't take out too much blood at once; so a rider using this method has to work to a timetable of blood bags out and blood bags in, to have enough ready to take them through a Grand Tour. It involves a lot of shuffling to the doctor to give blood – which can leave dopers with a lot of lying to do about their whereabouts, not to mention a big laundry bill. Hamilton describes coming back from one blood transfusion session to discover his sleeve soaked in blood and turning up at the airport 'looking like I'd just murdered someone.' Scientific tests aside, all of which leaves a trail (*see* below).

But just as the testers eventually caught up with EPO, so the use of blood transfusions became detectable. The introduction by the UCI of the Blood Passport in 2009, put a lot more information at the fingertips of the authorities: any anomalies in a rider's blood parameters could be spotted and checked. That, plus a more wide-reaching testing programme – with more out-of-season testing and riders having to inform the authorities of their whereabouts to the point that testers can turn up without warning at an hour's notice – has, one hopes, tilted the balance in favour of the authorities. Though if the history of cycling suggests anything, it is that this state of affairs won't last forever.

BIRILLO (SP)

In 2006, the Spanish police launched Operation Puerto against the team of Spanish doctors at the heart of the blood-doping programme that Tyler

Hamilton, among many other riders, was involved in. Raids on offices in Madrid produced the sort of stash that made the contents of Willy Voets' Fiat at the 1998 Tour look like small time. Here were over 200 bags of blood, plasma, refrigerators, coolers, over 100 assorted types of medication from Prozac to EPO, not to mention a paper trail of invoices, charge sheets, calendars and schedules. As Hamilton noted, this operation was less like 'a boutique service for elite riders' and more like 'Wal-Mart, servicing what seemed like half the peloton.'

The one problem for the authorities was exactly whose blood was whose. Each bag had a code for each different rider involved (and it wasn't just cyclists – athletes from other sports were involved too). Tyler Hamilton's code was 4142, which was the last four numbers of the phone number of a childhood friend. Then there was *hijo rudicio* or 'son of Rudy': this was Jan Ullrich, the 'Rudy' in question being his advisor, Rudy Pevenage. And there was the mysterious Birillo: this turned out to be Ivan Basso, who'd decided that his codename should be the name of his dog.

SUR UNE AUTRE PLANÈTE (FR)

At the 1999 Tour of Renewal, not everyone believed the fairytale story of Lance Armstrong's stunning return from cancer survivor to *maillot jaune*. After Armstrong won the first mountain stage to Sestrière, French papers like *L'Équipe* and *Le Monde* questioned his performance. *L'Équipe* described it as 'extraterrestrial' under the headline '*Sur Une Autre Planète*' – 'on another planet'. It didn't take a rocket scientist to work out what they were inferring.

Fast forward to the 2015 Tour and stage 10, where Chris Froome won the first mountain stage to La Pierre-Saint-Martin. It was a dominant, Tour-winning performance, with Froome putting a minute into Nairo Quintana, nearly three into Alberto Contador and four and a half into Vincenzo Nibali. But such is the current level of mistrust in cycling that any powerful performance is immediately questioned. In Froome's case, one of his accusers was Laurent Jalabert, the former rider turned television pundit. Jalabert, who retroactively tested positive for EPO in 2004, described himself as feeling 'uncomfortable' with Froome's winning margin, that it was 'surreal to see how superior Froome was' and – here's the clincher – that Froome was 'on another planet'.

By using that famous phrase, it was clear that Jalabert was making a comparison with Armstrong. It allowed him to float the suggestion that Froome's performance wasn't clean, but without the legally trickier bit of making the accusation direct. Later, when asked by reporters to substantiate the claims, Jalabert denied having made them, despite making them live on national television. The irony that riders such Froome were under suspicion because of the behaviour of other riders who had doped in the past was apparently lost on Jalabert.

THERAPEUTIC USE EXEMPTION (TUE)

When is taking drugs not taking drugs? When it is a Therapeutic Use Exemption, or TUE. TUEs are uses of certain drugs sanctioned by the cycling authorities to deal with medical conditions after a recommendation from a team doctor. Their use isn't made public, unless the rider chooses to tell the media. Or, in the case of Sir Bradley Wiggins, if a Russian group of hackers decide to release a load of medical records of Western sports stars to muddy the international waters over doping.

In 2016, four years after winning the Tour de France, the hacking group Fancy Bears released details of how Wiggins had been given a TUE by the authorities for the use of triamcinolone before the 2011 and 2012 Tour de Frances, and the 2013 Giro D'Italia. The reason for its use was to deal with pollen allergies, and hay fever in particular. Wiggins subsequently revealed he had been suffering with allergies since the 2003 Giro and thought they had been affecting his performance. Over the counter products such as Clarityn and nasal sprays weren't sufficient so in 2011 Team Sky sent him to see a specialist, who recommended applying for a TUE to have an injection of the corticosteroid triamcinolone to deal with the problem.

The problem with dealing with the problem, however, was threefold. Firstly, there no was no previous mention of Wiggins' ongoing struggle with pollen allergies, for example in his autobiography (in a 2016 interview he said he was 'paranoid about making excuses'). Secondly, Wiggins had also claimed in his autobiography that he had ascribed to British Cycling's 'no needle' policy, saying 'it was something I grew up with as a bike rider ... I've never had an injection, apart from I've had my injections, and on occasions have been put on a drip' (in 2016, he clarified his comments to say he was specifically talking about the 'illegal practice of intravenous injections of performance-enhancing subjects').

Thirdly, while triamcinolone is a drug that does deal with pollen allergies, it can also has the effect of allowing riders to lose weight while maintaining power. Wiggins argued in 2016 that the injections were actually 'a detriment to my performance', but other cyclists have experienced different results. It was one of the drugs that David Millar took before he was banned for doping in 2004, and he described the version he took, Kenacort, as the 'most potent' drug he had taken: 'if I took Kenacort, 1.5-2kgs would drop off in like a week. And not only would the weight drop off I would feel stronger.'

Wiggins and Team Sky did everything within the rules set out by the cycling authorities. But the way the story unfolded left the impression of a deliberate gaming of the system, and a form of marginal gains less fluffy than a personal pillow. Team Sky's image was further tarnished by accusations over a Jiffy Bag sent to Wiggins at the 2011 Critérium du Dauphiné, prior to the first TUE. In a 2017, a fourteen-month investigation by the UK Anti-Doping (UKAD) failed to reach a conclusion as to whether or not the parcel contained a banned substance. Team Sky claimed it contained the legal congestent Flumicil but were unable to provide any medical records to back this up: the team doctor, Richard Freeman, first failed to upload them to his computer, and then had his laptop stolen while on holiday in Greece. It left the episode with the unsatisfactory outcome of neither damning nor exonerating the participants.

Either way, all of this felt counter to the spirit of Team Sky's original goals of winning a Tour within five years and doing so cleanly. Some cyclists and commentators have since called for TUEs to be banned, to stop anyone gaining an advantage, whether deliberate or accidental. Others had argued for all TUEs to be made public. Yes, it's true that in a sport where drugs have long formed a dark part of its history, modern riders can sometimes feel as though they are cycling in the shadows of their predecessors. But that makes the case for transparency and openness all the more important, and this particular case all the more frustrating.

STICKY BOTTLE
La Bouteille Collante (Fr)

Ah, the humble *bidon*. Who knew that a bottle designed for providing water for a thirsty rider could have quite so many ingenious uses. As we have seen above, any number of riders preferred something a little stronger than *l'eau minerale* in their water bottle. But there were also riders who preferred something a little heavier in their drinks bottle, too. At the 1953 Tour, Jean Robic had his filled with lead, which he picked up at the top of climbs in order to help him speed down them faster on the other side.

But as well as being heavier and stronger, the humble water bottle has often turned out to be somewhat stickier. Right from the start of road racing, riders were not just getting tows but taking a train or jumping in a car, if they thought they could get away with it. It's a cycling tradition that Vincenzo Nibali did his best to continue at the 2015 Vuelta, holding on to a team car to move himself back up the race after a crash on the second stage. *If it wasn't for those damn pesky helicopter cameras…*

Nibali was disqualified from the race, though arguably his behavior was no worse than many other riders – just more blatant. In the case of a Sticky Bottle, a rider nominally goes back to the team car to pick up a *bidon*, but with rotten luck and misfortune, such is the 'stick' on the bottle that the person in the car can't let go and the rider ends up getting a pull up the road whilst the person in the car does his best to release it. A totally innocent situation that a passing *commissaire* might mistakenly translate as a rider getting a free ride.

A similar misunderstanding can occur with the use of a Magic Spanner – whereby a once speedy mechanic seems to take an age to fix a bike, hampering his poor rider who is desperate to get back to racing but has no choice but to hold on to the car while his bike is being fixed. (And on such a steep part of the climb as well: what rotten luck!)

'Any director would have done the same thing in our situation,' said Nibali's team manager after the disqualification. 'I've seen this a thousand times before at the Tour, everywhere.' 'What happens in the Vuelta happens in every race,' Nibali added. 'I'm not the first or the last in this type of story.'

BACKHANDERS

'Everyone knows that the greatest cycling champion can't ride alone. He needs a team. Yet there are still those who whisper, 'Yes, of course, so-and-so won because he "bought" such-and-such a rider. Once again, this is pure hypocrisy. It's quite clear that we "buy" riders and I say that it's quite normal.'

Just as he was upfront about the use of drugs in cycling, so Jacques Anquetil was also pretty straight about the deal-making that goes on, as in this newspaper article from 1967. Perhaps more so than *dopage*, the practice of paying cyclists from other teams to help a rider's cause has long been the great unspoken of bike racing. It's a subject where the *omerta* of the peloton pulls down the shutters and the outside world is afforded only glimpses of the practice.

Paying riders for services has a long history. Maurice Brocco was disqualified from the 1911 Tour for selling his services as a pacer to other riders once he was out of the running for the overall classification. In the 1950s, Federico Bahamontes felt he lost a number of races because other teams had colluded against him. Others, such as Bernardo Ruiz agreed that he suffered from not paying out: 'Bahamontes wouldn't spend anything to gain the team's sympathy,' he says of the 1957 Spanish squad for the Vuelta, in which he famously lost out to Jesús Loroño and found himself isolated in the peloton.

Raymond Poulidor made similar claims after he lost to Jacques Anquetil in the 1966 Paris–Nice. For once in first place after beating *Monsieur Chrono* (*see also* Chapter Ten) in the time-trial, Poulidor lost out on the final stage after concerted attacks by a number of teams. Paul Howard quotes Philippe Brunel on the subject in his biography of Anquetil: 'There were two managers – agents if you like – in France. Roger Piel and and Daniel Dousset. Dousset had Anquetil, Bitossi, Aimar, Altig and Adorni. Alliances in the peloton were arranged by the managers, not between the teams... In this Paris–Nice, there was Adorni, who raced for Anquetil because Dousset told him he had to. He said, "I need to maintain Anquetil's prestige for the criteriums."'

In 1985, Robert Millar lost out in the Vuelta to Pedro Delgado, partly because of being on the wrong side of the arrangements. 'If I'd known then what I do now,' Millar said afterwards, 'I would have reached some agreements.' Though rather than being a rider's responsibility, this was something for the *directeur sportif* to sort – in this case Peugeot team manager Roland Berland. 'It's kind of common knowledge in Europe that other teams can be bought to give you help in certain races,' Millar later expanded. 'It's up to the *directeur sportif* to deal with these kinds of matters.' Berland didn't, and left his rider exposed as a result. Sean Yates, one of Millar's teammates, put it succinctly in Richard Moore's biography of Millar: 'Berland was a fucking idiot.'

When Charly Wegelius was offered money to help the Italian team at the 1995 Worlds, he was far from the first person to be put in such a position. Tom Simpson, who won Britain's first rainbow jersey in 1965, admitted in an article for the *People* newspaper that he had offered the Irish rider Shay Elliot £1,100 to help him win the title in 1963. Indeed, the Worlds in particular is rife with stories of titles being bought – that crossover of conflicts between team and country making riders particularly susceptible to helping others out.

How much of this behaviour still continues is unclear. But as with doping, not making current headlines shouldn't be taken as proof that racing is now clean of such practices.

FOURTEEN | The Races of Races

Every race on the cycling calendar is special in its own individual way. But some editions of each event stand out more than others, capturing something about the sport that stands the test of time – for better of for worse. Welcome, then, to a selection of the best of the best, and in some unfortunate cases, the worst of the worst that cycling history has to offer.

THE 1914 GIRO D'ITALIA
Il Più Duro di Tutti (It)/'The Toughest of Them All'

There are hard Grand Tours. And there are hard Grand Tours. And there is the 1914 Giro d'Italia, sometimes called *Il Più Duro di Tutti*: 'The Toughest of Them All'. Eight stages with an average length of 395 kilometres. Terrible weather. A race so severe that 90 per cent of its competitors failed to make it to the finish. The number of riders who crossed the line was just eight. Eight.

The 420-kilometre opening stage from Milan to Cuneo didn't so much sort out the men from the boys as the foolhardy from the sensible. Setting off at midnight – night starts were the norm for such long stages – the riders got a full fifteen minutes of riding in before the heavens opened. It seriously rained – a torrential downpour that wouldn't let up for the next 36 hours. With no streetlighting, the riders rode through the night in complete darkness. Next up were the nails strewn across the road at Arona, thought to have been spread by disgruntled locals. Having mended their punctures, the riders reached daylight to discover that the storm had blown the race signage away, and many headed off in the wrong direction. The roads were reduced to 'a river of mud' according to one account: the riders were caked in it and beginning to look like the living dead.

It was too much for double Tour winner, Lucien Petit-Breton (so called because there was another cyclist named Lucien Breton and he was, well, smaller). As Petit-Breton fixed his nth puncture in the bucketing rain, he asked his team car for a clean jersey, only to be told that because of the weather he'd gone through the entire supply and they had no spares left. In true Basil Fawlty style, he took about attacking the car, before cycling off in a huff, bare-chested, before abandoning.

Petit-Breton wasn't the only one. In fact, 60 per cent of the field abandoned, and the race organizers dropped their plans for time limits to stop more riders from leaving (only 24 made it inside the cut). And it wasn't as if it was a weak field: the winners of all five of the previous Giros were taking part, as well as the entire top ten riders from the previous year's race. But even the hardest of riders were broken by that first stage. Luigi Ganna, the first winner of the Giro and nicknamed The King of the Mud, ended up sobbing uncontrollably as the torrential rain turned into a blizzard. Angelo Gremo finally won the stage, arriving in Cueno at 5.30pm. The last finisher didn't make it in until after midnight.

The weather and the attrition continued. A blizzard during stage 6 led to the race leader, Giuseppi Azzini, disappearing. He was eventually found a couple of days later by a farmer, who found Azzini holed up in one of his barns with a high temperature. The eventual race leader of this remarkable event was Alfonso Calzolari: such were the time gaps that he won the race despite having been given a three-hour penalty for taking a lift through the mountains.

THE 1946 GIRO D'ITALIA
Il Giro della Rinascita (It)/'The Giro of Rebirth'

The first Giro after the Second World War was one of its most memorable three times over. A year before the restart of the Tour, Il Giro della Rinascita took place in a land ravaged by fighting and amongst a population coming to terms with the events of the previous five years. As John Foot writes in *Pedlare! Pedlare!*: 'homelessness was rife and people lived in shacks or even caves. Life was hard and many Italians were reduced to living from hand to mouth. Criminal behaviour reached an all-time high, particularly in 1946. The prisons were overflowing and riots spread like wildfire up and down the country.'

In this context, running the 1946 Giro was seen as a way to help unite the country; to get the people to look forward rather than back, to give them something to cheer for in these darkest of days. The effects of the war, of course, were everywhere. The route largely avoided the south of the country, such was the devastation to the roads and railways, though there were more than enough reminders of action on the rest of the route from Naples to Cassino – two cities heavily hit by allied bombing. The riders, too, needed to recover from their own experiences of war: Fausto Coppi had been a POW in North Africa, cycling back to the north of Italy following his return to Naples; some, like Fiorenzo Magni, were excluded for fighting for the fascists during the war.

But it wasn't just the politics of the past that the 1946 Giro had to overcome. Stage 12 was set to run from Rovigo to Trieste: a finish in a city whose ownership was very much in dispute. As the Iron Curtain descended across Europe, Trieste was one of the flashpoints during the opening days of the Cold War: both Italy and Yugoslavia's General Tito were laying claim, with Slavic forces having taken control of the city in the aftermath of the end of the war.

To take the Giro d'Italia to Trieste was a high-risk decision. The race organizers first rerouted the finish to safer territory in Vittorio Veneto, then restored the original plan after concerns that Trieste could riot if the race didn't come there. On the stage itself, the riders found themselves ambushed by local Slavs and the race ground to a halt, first, under a hail of stones and then under gunfire. The peloton was split: some didn't want to continue, others like Trieste-born Giordano Cottur insisted the race go ahead. The upshot was that the stage was officially annulled, with most of the riders heading on to Udine for the next stage. But a hardy band of riders, led by Cottur, climbed into army trucks and were driven past further ambushes – everything from mines to barbed wire – before restarting the race on the outskirts of Trieste. Cottur, fittingly, went on to win the 'stage'. (Trieste, after a period as a 'free territory', remained Italian.)

The 1946 Giro is also remembered for a third reason: it was the start of one of cycling's epic rivalries, between Gino Bartali and his former *gregari* (*see domestique*, Chapter Three), Fausto Coppi. Fittingly for such a charged Giro, the race had a battle for the *maglia rosa* (*see* Chapter Five) that it deserved – an epic duel, with Bartali coming out on top by just 47 seconds. For those few glorious weeks, the Giro did what its organizers had intended: allowed Italy to forget about its troubles and challenges and lose itself in the beauty of the sport.

THE 1947 TOUR DE FRANCE
The Tour of Liberation
The Tour de France restarted one year after the Giro, in 1947. Sometimes called the Tour of Liberation, the Tour started its post-war life with a new

Above A helping hand for Jean Robic at the 1947 Tour de France

director, Jacques Goddet (Desgrange had died in 1940), and a new organization (*L'Équipe* and *Le Parisien Libéré*). Goddet promised a race that would send 'a message of joy and confidence... a heroic adventure from which hatred is absent.' As with the 1946 Giro, the sights of war were everywhere: a number of the Tour stages followed the routes of the Allied armies as they liberated France.

Certainly France was ready for the Tour to restart. Post-war shortages of food and petrol were such that it looked as if the Tour organization would not be allowed enough provisions of either to run the race. At which point, dock-workers threatened to strike unless the petrol was handed over and the race was allowed to go ahead. The authorities relented.

As with the 1946 Giro, the 1947 Tour did much to reunite the country: a crowd of 300,000 turned out to watch the Tour set off from the Arc de Triomphe. Many were rooting for 'King' René Vietto, one of the few riders in the race to have ridden the Tour before. Vietto was perhaps more popular with the fans than with his fellow cyclists, given his habit of slapping riders across the face if they tried to escape from the peloton. Vietto, though, lost the *maillot jaune* with two days to go to Pierre Brambilla, a rider born in Switzerland but riding for the Italian team. Brambilla went into the final day in yellow and, according to tradition, shouldn't have been attacked. But the young French rider Jean Robic had other ideas and broke away with Edouard Fachleitner: with war memories lingering on, Brambilla could get no help from the peloton to bring him back. Depending on which account you read, Robic either paid Fachleitner to help him win, or the pair used photographer's motorbikes to illegally slipstream for much of the escape. Whatever the truth, Robic rode to victory to the delight of the whole country – the first rider to do so having never worn the yellow jersey during the rest of the race. Brambilla was so distraught at losing that, according to cycling legend, he cut up his bike and buried it in the garden.

THE 1949 TOUR DE FRANCE
Il Tour Degla Imbroglio (It)/'The Tour of Trickery'

By 1949, Fausto Coppi versus Gino Bartali was one of cycling's – indeed, sport's – great rivalries. Which was fine when they competed for different teams, such as in the Giro, but a more complicated scenario when they had to appear on the same side. At the 1948 World Championships at Valkenberg in the Netherlands, the pair had been uncooperative to the point of marking each other during the race, with both banned by the Italian cycling authorities for their behaviour.

So with the 1949 Tour de France set to include national rather than trade teams, team manager Alfreda Binda had his work cut out. A truce was negotiated prior to the race: rather than having one leader, the Italian team would split down the middle, with each rider bringing five *gregari* (*see domestique*, Chapter Three) each. The riders were to help each other out until the mountains, at which point whichever rider was stronger would take over. To keep the team together, amid claim and counterclaim, Binda needed to deploy every diplomatic trick in the book.

When Coppi crashed on stage 5 and the replacement bike was the wrong size, Binda had to both persuade Coppi not to quit the race and Bartali to wait for him. Mistrust was everywhere. Coppi thought he'd been given the wrong replacement bike because Binda and Bartali were in cahoots. Bartali, meanwhile, was cross with Binda for bending over backwards to keep Coppi in the race – depriving him, as he saw it, of a potential Tour win. On the mountainous stage 16 from Cannes to Briançon, the pair broke free then began to do their 1948 World Championship watching-each-other thing again, until Binda threatened them with large fines if they didn't start racing. As the breakaway continued, Coppi fell off and Bartali punctured, but both waited for the other. Bartali went on to win the stage and took the yellow jersey.

The following day, Bartali first punctured, then crashed on the decent of the Grand St Bernard. Coppi slowed to wait for Bartali, but this time Binda told him to go on, and it was Coppi's turn to take the stage and yellow jersey (Bartali fans dispute that Binda gave Coppi the signal to go). Even so, Coppi still didn't completely trust Binda: he'd keep hold of the notes of the time gaps that Binda gave him during the race, to doublecheck them against the official results at the end of the day. That Binda overcame such mistrust and rivalry to ensure a win for the Italian team was a testament to his people skills.

THE 1957 VUELTA A ESPAÑA
The 'Pact of Huesca'

The rivalry between Federico Bahamontes and Jesús Loroño was more complicated than that of Coppi and Bartali (*see* above). There was professional rivalry for sure – Loroño had won the King of the Mountains category in the 1953 Tour, Bahamontes had succeeded him in 1954. But there were political and social elements thrown into the mix too. Bahamontes was from Toledo, near the Spanish capital of Madrid; Loroño was from the Basque country. Finally, rather than having a team leader like Alfreda Binda, the pair rode for the Spanish national team at the 1957 Vuelta under Luis Puig – a man lacking Binda's diplomatic skills and essentially unequipped to deal with such a rivalry.

As with the 1949 Tour, the 1957 Vuelta exposed the difficulty of having two fierce rivals competing in the same team. Unlike the 1949 Tour, the balance of the team was more decisively tipped in one rider's favour: a number of those selected were from the Faema squad, teammates of another Bahamontes rival, Bernardo Ruiz (Ruiz hadn't been selected for the national squad but headed up the Mediterranean regional team instead). Bahamontes took the race lead first, but lost it when the team failed to tell him the size of the gap gained by a breakaway – only finding out from the race organizers and reacting when it was too late. He fought his way back into the race lead, pulling clear of Loroño by eleven minutes and Puig announced to the press that Bahamontes was now the team leader and his rival would be going for the King of the Mountains instead.

But on the stage to Tortosa, Loroño and Bernardo Ruiz attacked. There are differing accounts of the action taken by Bahamontes' team and manager to stop him responding. Some accounts suggest that Puig blocked the road with his car to let Loroño escape; others claim that Bahamontes' teammates held on to his shorts to stop him riding after his rival; more prosaically, it is claimed that Puig drove off after the breakaway, ordering the team not to chase it down. Certainly, Bahamontes found no support among his fellow riders – he ended the day six minutes behind the new race leader, Loroño, and three behind Ruiz.

At dinner, Bahamontes let his feelings be known; Loroño responded to the tirade of insults by grabbing Bahamontes by the shirt and asking him what his problem was. Bahamontes left and had his meal sent up to him, claiming he felt threatened by Loroño. The next day, Bahamontes attacked; Loroño responded, and the two rode together, shouting and arguing, even after other riders had taken advantage to break ahead of them. At the following stage, a time-trial from Zaragoza to Huesca, the rivalry continued with Loroño beating Bahamontes by just six seconds.

At which point, the Spanish Cycling Federation stepped in. They sent a telegram to Puig telling him that unless the two riders stopped their public feud, they would both be excluded from the race. According to Alistair Fotheringham's *The Eagle of Toledo*, Puig apparently told Bahamontes, *sotto voce*, that if Loroño did not win the Vuelta, 'there was no way either he or Bahamontes would be allowed inside Bilbao [where the race finished].'

Whatever the truth, the result was the 'Pact of Huesca', in which the rivals shook hands for the cameras and the Spanish team drank a toast to loyalty and unity. 'We have seen how Loroño and Bahamontes shook hands as a sign of victory and friendship while a band played a series of military marches', reported *La Vanguardia*. It was a sop to satisfy the authorities: Bahamontes continued to attack, winning the King of the Mountains, but Loroño, Ruiz and their riders were too strong for him to do anything about the overall lead.

THE 1967 OTLEY '12'

Beryl Burton's record as a cyclist is an extraordinary one, but even in her remarkable palmarès, the events of 17 September 1967 stand out.

This was the date of the Otley '12' – a twelve-hour time-trial against the clock: whoever rode the furthest was the winner. It's a challenge about many things: ability, yes, but also endurance, determination and grit. The contestants had set off at two-minute intervals. The 99th to go at 7.10 was Mike McNamara, who far from being a cycling slouch, was in fact the favourite to take the accoloade for that year's Best All Rounder. Beryl began two minutes later, her initial aim of beating her 1959 record of 250.37 miles.

In 1967, she was to go somewhat better. Over a course that took particpants around various Yorkshire A-roads for just over 200 miles, before a looping finishing circuit of just under 16 miles, Burton managed to keep McNamara in her sights. After 100 miles, she was 57 seconds slower than him; after 160 miles she was level; at 200 miles she was 18 seconds up. Other riders by this point had already been overtaken by the pair. Keith Lambert, who was to finish eighth, was passed early on – according to William Fotheringham's biography of Burton, she said something along the lines of 'Come on lad, what are you doing?' as she went past.

It was on the finishing circuit that Burton really put the hammer down. She gained 42 seconds on McNamara on the first lap; towards the end of the second lap, she was in a position to overtake him. Fotheringham's biography quotes Beryl's infamous response: 'He was weaving a little so I thought, "I'll offer him one of my favourites." I got out a packet of liquorice allsorts, tore off the top and offered Mac one, which he took. He took the best one, the sort with the coconut around the liquorice.'

In total, Burton went on to cycle 277.25 miles, finishing 45 seconds before the end of the 12 hours because she felt she'd done enough. She certainly had: Burton had broken the overall record for the discipline, which had stood for nine years. It would be another two years before a man could better her time; she still holds the women's record, even today.

THE 1968 TOUR DE FRANCE
Tour de Santé (Fr)/'The Healthy Tour'

Tom Simpson wasn't the first cyclist to die during a Tour de France. That macabre honour rests with Francisco Cepeda, who died after a fall on the Galibier at the 1935 Tour. But Simpson's death on the slopes of Mont Ventoux was the first – and possibly only – death during the Tour, or any other professional cycling race, to be drugs related. His use of amphetamines, combined with the searing temperatures on the slopes of the Ventoux, was too much for his body to take.

The following year, the Tour called itself the *Tour de Santé* – 'The Healthy Tour'. To emphasize the point, it began in the spa town of Vittel, famous for its mineral water. It might have just been coincidence, but in a TV debate with a government minister, Jacques Anquetil once famously asked, 'You think you can ride Bordeaux–Paris on just mineral water?' Indeed, 'not riding on mineral water' has become one of those slang terms for doping.

Drugs and cycling didn't end their relationship in 1968 of course, despite race director Jacques Goddet's claim that, 'Doping is no longer a mysterious sickness, hidden, uncontrollable, uncontrolled. It really seems that there is a common determination among the riders to be rid of this scourge.' The main difference was that the authorities, rather than turning a blind eye, began to take a more pro-active line in testing. This had begun prior to Simpson's death, with anti-doping laws passed in France in 1965 and the impromptu testing of Raymond Poulidor, among others, at the 1966 Tour. The riders had reacted angrily to this new imposition, walking a section of the following stage and shouting complaints. By 1968, however, the mood music had changed: the UCI had introduced penalties for doping in November 1967, with a month's suspension for a first offence and life for multiple offenders. Whether the attitude of the riders themselves had really changed is a moot point, but the *contrôle anti-dopage* van was now a fixture of each stage finish.

As for the 1968 Tour itself, it was one of those transitional years, prior to the start of the Eddy Merckx era in 1969. With almost predictable bad luck, Raymond Poulidor was unable to take advantage of a peloton lacking either The Cannibal or the now-declining Jacques Anquetil, abandoning after crashing while trying to avoid a motorcycle. It the was Dutchman Jan Janssen who emerged victorious – the first Dutch rider to win the race.

THE 1980 LIÈGE–BASTOGNE–LIÈGE
Neige –Bastogne –Neige (Fr)

In *The Monuments*, Peter Cossins describes the 1980 edition of Liège–Bastogne–Liège as 'perhaps the single most discussed and written about Classic in racing history.' It was 'less a race than a fight for survival,' William Fotheringham notes in his biography of the winner, Bernard Hinault. Certainly, it was one of the most stunning victories of one of cycling's greatest ever riders.

What made Liège–Bastogne–Liège in 1980 so memorable was the weather – the snow, as the edition's nickname so wittily records. Such were the conditions that some riders collected their numbers but never made it to the start line. That leads to various accounts of exactly how many riders quit the race: what is undisputed is that out of a field of 170-odd, only 21 made it to the finish, with over half the riders having abandoned before even a third of the course was completed. Conditions were appalling. The snow was so deep that the riders could only cycle in the tyre tracks left by the race cars. In Fotheringham's Hinault biography, Sean Kelly describes how one of his teammates was so cold he couldn't get his clothes off back at the hotel and just climbed into the bath with everything on; when it was Hinault's turn for a dip, he had to have a cold bath because a hot one was too painful.

Hinault was tough, but he was not a rider who enjoyed the conditions – in fact, he had a dislike for the cold and the wet. Yet a mixture of pride, the weather and some adroit management from Cyrille Guimard kept him going. With his teammate Maurice Le Guilloux in the race, Hinault felt that he couldn't quit and that as team leader, he had to be the last man standing. Then Hinault said he'd abandon if it was still snowing by the time he got to the feeding station: briefly, the clouds paused. Finally, Guimard's encouragement and a supply of fresh equipment kept him going; Guimard told Hinault to take off his rain-jacket, forcing him to ride harder to keep warm.

Hinault found himself out front and alone with 80 kilometres of the race to go. 'I didn't look at anything. I saw nothing. I only thought of myself,' he said later. He won the race by nine and a half minutes from Hennie Kuiper, with the last of the finishers coming in 25 minutes later. It was a great, heroic win and the sort that is less likely to happen today – if those conditions occurred now, the race would surely be postponed. But it was a victory that came at a cost for Hinault: his fingers have remained sensitive to the cold ever since. Fotheringham, too, cites Philippe Brunel's theory that Hinault's later knee problems can be traced back to riding that race without any protection on his legs.

THE 1982 WORLD CHAMPIONSHIPS
La Fucilata di Goodwood (It)/'The Goodwood Rifle Shot'

In his history of the Giro d'Italia *Maglia Rosa,* Herbie Sykes describes the strengths of Italian rider Guiseppi Saronni as being 'lightning fast in a sprint, exceptional against the watch, tidy in the hills.' It was a combination that saw him win two Grand Tours (the Giro in 1979 and 1983), one Monument (the 1983 Milan–San Remo) and the rainbow jersey at the 1982 World Championships.

The Worlds that year were held in the UK at Goodwood in Sussex. The 9.5-mile circuit used the motor-racing track there, as well as the South Downs countryside, to create a course that Sean Kelly described in his memoir as 'not hugely selective'. There was a hill towards the end of the circuit, which hit ten

Above Bernard Hinault versus the
elements, 1980 Liège-Bastogne-Liège

per cent at the one-kilometre-to-go mark – meaning that either a bunch
sprint or a breakaway was unlikely. Kelly's feeling was that it would come down
to 'a sprint between a small group', which would suit him. Which it did – with a
third place finish, despite the fact that the Irish team consisted of just him and
Stephen Roche.

The two main players in the race were the Americans and the Italians. The
US had nine places but only filled six, as riders had to pay their own way. Even
the six-man team was a team in name only. Jonathan Boyer was the most
experienced, being the first American rider to take part in the Tour de France
in 1981; but coming up fast was the young Greg LeMond, who had his own
plans for glory. So when Boyer made the decisive move from the slimmed-
down peloton on the final lap, it was his teammate LeMond who chased him
down, dragging the winning rider across with him.

The full-strength Italian team were full of stars such as Moreno Argentin,
Francesco Moser and Pierino Gavazzi, but it was to be Saronni's day. As Boyer
was caught, Saronni launched his sprint – one of those quite remarkable bursts
of speed that leaves all the other cyclists looking as though they are riding
backwards. 'It was as if he'd been fired from a cannon', recalled Kelly; 'an
antelope-like leap,' described journalist Bruno Raschi; 'one of the most
magnificent moments in the history of modern cycling,' according to one
proud Italian newspaper. There might be a touch of partisan reporting, but
even so, *la fucilata* – the rifleshot – is one of cycling's special moments.

THE 1989 VUELTA A ESPAÑA
The 'White Envelope Scandal'

The 1989 Vuelta was a battle between Pedro 'Perico' Delgado, winner of the 1985 Vuelta and 1988 Tour de France, and Fabio Parra from Colombia, who'd come third in the 1988 Tour. A popular figure in his native Spain, Delgado was a rider whose victories seemed to go hand in hand with controversy. At the 1985 Vuelta, he took the race lead on the final mountain stage from Robert Millar, with the Scot first unaware of Delgado's escape and then, when he was told, finding that the Spanish riders in the peloton were willing to sacrifice their own chances for a homegrown victory. However, at the 1988 Tour de France, Delgado tested positive for probenecid, a well-known masking agent for steroids, that was on the Olympic banned list but not yet on the UCI's.

The 1989 Vuelta was no different. As with the 1985 race, the crucial final mountain stage saw the race go to Segovia, Delgado's home town. This time it was Delgado defending the leader's jersey, and Parra made a serious fist of taking it back. He broke clear of Delgado on the Navacerrada and crossed the gap to join his teammate, Omar Hernández, who'd been sent ahead for such a purpose. The gap back to Delgado, now shorn of *domestiques* (*see* Chapter Three), was so large that Parra was the virtual leader on the road. But then Delgado found unlikely support from the young Russian rider, Ivan Ivanov. Ivanov was riding for a rival team, but helped Delgado reduce the gap and stay in yellow. It had been the second occasion during the race that Ivanov had helped Delgado: earlier, on stage 14, Parra had again tried to drop Delgado, only for Ivanov to help Delgado back again.

At the start of the final stage, Delgado was filmed handing over a white envelope to Ivanov, who pocketed it. What was in the white envelope became the subject of claim and counterclaim. In the Colombian media, the implication was that Delgado had paid Ivanov to help him – it was suggested that the envelope contained $2,500. Delgado's response was that the envelope contained nothing more than his address: he and Ivanov had become friends and the Russian might want to look him up next time he was in town. Aw.

True or not, this heartwarming tale of Spanish-Russian friendship was not bought back in Colombia. As with Robert Millar in 1985, the sense of a stitch up and being cheated out of the race lingered on – a legitimate claim or otherwise. For the Colombians, the white envelope was proof that Parra should have won the race, rather than lose it by 35 seconds. It would be another 25 years before a Colombian won a Grand Tour – though Nairo Quintana's victory, ironically, was not without a touch of its own controversy.

THE 1998 TOUR DE FRANCE
L'Affaire Festina/ Tour de Farce/Tour du Doping

It's not cheap to sponsor a cycling team. But companies stump up the money for prestige purposes, for the associations that having their name on a cycling jersey brings, and to bask in the collective glory of team victory. Pity poor Festina, then – the Spanish watchmaking firm whose name will be forever synonymous with one of the biggest drug scandals in cycling history.

On Wednesday 8 July, a few days before the start of the 1998 Tour, the Festina *soigneur* (*see* Chapter Eight) Willy Voet was stopped at the French-Belgian border. He was driving a white Fiat – a regulation team car, complete with logos – which he had picked up in Issy-les-Molineaux and then driven from France to Switzerland to Germany to Belgium. Returning to France, Voet had turned off the main E17 motorway and entered the country on a quieter, usually unpatrolled road.

In this instance, however, Voet was stopped and the border guards discovered a stash and a half of chemical goodies: EPO, growth hormones, testosterone and blood-thinning tablets. There were enough capsules and doses and bottles to open up a pharmacy. Either that or, well, to power a cycling team through a three-week Grand Tour. To begin with, Voet tried to claim that the drugs were for his own personal use. The team *directeur sportif* (*see* Chapter Eight) Bruno Roussel denied knowing anything about it. The Tour de France director, Jean-Marie Leblanc, getting ready for the start of the Tour in Ireland, suggested that it wasn't directly connected to the race.

But then Voet confessed. Roussel was also arrested, along with the team doctor, Eric Ryckaert. As the truth slowly emerged of a team-supervised doping programme, Leblanc threw the entire Festina team out of the race, which included such big names as Alex Zülle and Richard Virenque. The riders threatened to turn up and ride anyway, but were dissuaded. As the arrests and raids continued, a number of other teams also left the race. The riders who remained – and only about half reached Paris – staged strikes in response to the way that they were being treated by the police, who were raiding the teams at night and taking them to nearby hospitals for tests.

The 'race' was 'won' by Marco Pantani, who in 2013 was among the riders whose 1998 urine samples showed traces of EPO, when tested retroactively (Pantani was also disqualified from the following year's Giro for having a hematocrit count over the regulation 50, a sign of suspected EPO use). All of which seems fitting, somehow: Festina were the ones who were caught, but how many other members of the peloton were also using EPO... only they know. Over ten years on, *L'Affaire Festina* loses little of its shock value, though – given the history of the sport – this is unlikely to be the last case of its kind.

THE 1999 TOUR DE FRANCE
The Tour of Renewal

Just as the death of Tom Simpson in 1967 was followed by the Healthy Tour, so the Tour du Doping was followed by the Tour of Renewal. This was the Tour's chance to redeem itself, to show the world that cycling had moved on from *L'Affaire Festina* and to allow fans to fall in love with the sport all over again.

Lance Armstrong was a rider with an extraordinary story to tell. 'Fifteen or 20 years ago I wouldn't be alive, much less starting the Tour de France,' he told a press conference during the race. Armstrong had been diagnosed with advanced testicular cancer in 1996; a cancer that had spread in his body to his lungs and brain. His chances of making it through were low – doctors gave him a 40 per cent chance of survival; but survive Armstrong did. He underwent chemotherapy and not only recovered against the odds but also managed to return to professional cycling.

Armstrong hadn't taken part in the 1998 Tour (his first Grand Tour post-cancer was that year's Vuelta, where he finished fourth). Instead, he followed the Tour from the TV commentary box and watched as *L'Affaire Festina* unfolded: 'Doping is an unfortunate fact of life in cycling,' he wrote in his bestselling memoir *It's Not About The Bike*. 'Some teams and riders feel it's like nuclear weapons – that they have to do it to stay competitive within the peloton. I never felt that way, and certainly after chemo the idea of putting anything foreign in my body was especially repulsive.'

Right from the start of the 1999 Tour, Armstrong dominated the race. He won the opening prologue in Le Puy du Foy, and his victories in the two longer time-trials, as well as the opening Alpine mountain stage from Le Grand-Bornard to Sestrière, went on to cement his lead. By the time the race reached Paris, he was over seven minutes ahead of the second-placed rider, Alex Zülle.

For Lance Armstrong to return to the pinnacle of his sport after such a life-threatening illness was a remarkable achievement. After the damage that the Festina Affair had done to the image of the sport, his victory in the Tour of Renewal offered the world a new chapter in the race's long history. As race director Jean-Luc Leblanc said, 'Armstrong beating his illness is a sign that the Tour can beat its own illness.'

'After crossing the finish line,' Armstrong's teammate Tyler Hamilton remembered later in his memoir, 'we made that traditional ride down the Champs-Élysées, saw the Arc de Triomphe surrounded by a massive crowd waving American and Texas flags, got off our bikes and wandered around the cobblestones in happy disbelief, hugging our wives, our families, each other. I remember champagne bottles popping, a million flashbulbs going off, a guy in the crowd playing a tuba. It felt like we were inside a Hollywood movie.'

THE 2010 TOUR DE FRANCE
Chaingate

The etiquette of road racing is quite simple. The unspoken rule is that if the race leader is in trouble with a puncture or a mechanical, you don't attack. If they puncture, then their rivals should wait for them to recover before resuming battle.

That wasn't what happened at stage 15 of the 2010 Tour. On the slopes of the Port de Balès in the Pyrenees, *maillot jaune* (*see* Chapter Five) Andy Schleck attacked… then his chain came off. His rival, Alberto Contador, who had responded to Schleck's attack, didn't wait. Instead, he continued to put the pedal down and to put 39 seconds into his rival – exactly the time margin of his later overall win of the Tour.

It is one of the curiosities of cycling that in an era when doping was bending the sport to its limits, what really got cycling fans going was whether Contador should have waited while Schleck put his chain back on. 'My stomach is full of anger,' Schleck said afterwards. 'I would not have raced like that and taken advantage of the situation. For sure, those guys don't get the fair play prize today.'

Contador started by claiming he was unaware of what had happened to Schleck, which in this TV-camera, radio-earpieced age seems unlikely. Later, after being booed by fans on the podium, he apologized: 'The race was in full gear and, well, maybe I made a mistake. I'm sorry.' But even when he was being contrite, his competitive instinct was clear: 'I'd like to take the *maillot jaune* in different circumstances, but what's more important is that I took time. The race was on – you cannot stop the race at a moment like that.'

That ruthlessness is probably why Contador won seven Grand Tours prior to his retirement in 2017 and Schleck 'one'. Although Contador went on to finish in Paris 39 seconds ahead of his rival, he was subsequently stripped of his title after being tested positive for clenbuterol/eating a contaminated piece of steak for his supper. 'It doesn't feel like a proper victory,' said Schleck, on being handed the yellow jersey almost two years later; a comment that would have been equally at home if the original result had stood.

THE 2019 WORLD CHAMPIONSHIPS
The Yorkshire Worlds

You can't have a rainbow, so the song goes, without a little rain. Or to update it for the 2019 World Championships, you can't have a rainbow jersey without surviving a downpour of the stuff.

In 2019, the Worlds returned to the UK for the first time since the Goodwood Rifle Shot of 1982. This time, the setting was Yorkshire, with Harrogate the hub of the action. From a standing start, God Own's Country had quickly become part of the cycling establishment: the Tour de France in 2014, it's own Tour de Yorkshire now a fixture on the calendar, and now to top it all the host of the World Championships.

Unfortunately, it rained. A lot. And then it rained again some more. In the men's Under-23 time trial, Johan Price-Pejtersen of Denmark achieved internet notoriety for attempting and failing to traverse a road doing an impression of a small lake, while another puddle took out Hungarian Attila Valter, leaving him to aquaplane down the road on his backside. The supposed race highlight, the Men's Road Race, was another damp squib, with the weather forcing the removal of Buttertubs Pass and Grinton Moor, the two climbs where much of the race's action was expected to take place. In fact, throughout a soggy week, there was only one day of decent weather for cycling – the Saturday of the Women's Road Race.

Annemiek van Vleuten's expectations of success were limited before the start: in the time trial earlier in the week, she'd trailed in third in a competition she'd expected to win. But just 40 km into the race, van Vleuten had attacked on the climb of Lofthouse: 'I sped up and all of a sudden it got quiet around me,' she told *ProCycling* Magazine. 'I could still hear the crowds but not the noises of gears changing, or the other riders breathing. That's when I knew it was alone.'

It was a long way to the finish: 106 km to be precise. Van Vleuten shouldn't have had a hope in hell of staying out, but as the peloton split behind her, she matched the elite chasing group, holding a 50 second lead for mile after mile. Van Vleuten was helped by a mixture of the rival teams not pulling together to organize a chase, and also the strength of the Dutch team: her compatriots Anna van der Breggan and Marianne Vos sat in the second and third groups on the road, refusing to chase their teammate and biding their time. But ultimately, the victory was hers, holding her nerve and keeping going on an attack she knew should never have worked. Having spent over 100 km out in front on her own, van Vleuten won by two minutes from van der Breggan and over five minutes clear of what remained of the peloton.

THE 2020 TOUR DE FRANCE
The Tour de Covid

It was during the UEA Tour in late February that it first became apparent that the Coronavirus pandemic was going to make 2020 a cycling year like no other. Following positive tests on two Italian staff members of one of the teams, authorities cancelled the final two stages of the race, leaving participants and journalists following the race quarantined in a nearby hotel. A week later, the 2020 Paris-Nice was also curtailed in both length and size: Astana, Team Ineos, Movistar and Team Jumbo-Visma among those who pulled out.

As the pandemic took hold across Europe and the world, the cycling season ground to a halt. For a while, it looked as though that might be it for 2020. But as professional sport began to return, questions started being asked when and if cycling could restart. While some sports such as domestic football leagues could be more straightforwardly 'bubbled', cycling felt a different beast: an event like the Tour de France, which brings participants from across the world and then takes them all around the country, felt somewhat borderline. When the race began in Nice on 29 August, journalists following the race put its chances of reaching Paris at no more than 50-50.

And yet, not only did the Tour finish, but it served up one of the most exciting races in years. Before the start, all the talk was of a duel between Team Ineos and Team Jumbo-Visma. But first Chris Froome and Geraint Thomas were dropped from Ineos after poor form in the *Dauphine*. That just left Egan Bernal, but back and knee problems left him withdrawing almost twenty minutes behind *maillot jaune* Primoz Roglic. Going into the final time trial, the only person within a minute of the lead was Roglic's fellow Slovenian Tadej Pogacar. Pogacar had matched Roglic in the mountains, but had lost crucial time in echelon splits early on.

The final time trial took the riders from Lure to a finish at the top of La Planche des Belles Filles. Roglic can time trial – he has even won silver in the discipline at the World Championships. And his time that Saturday wasn't terrible: he still finished fifth on the stage. Rather, it was Pogacar's ride up the final climb that made the stage one for the record books. Over the first 30 km, he had clawed back 36 seconds of Roglic's lead. But on those last six kilometres he gained another 80 seconds to reach the finish line in a satisfyingly even 55 minutes and 55 seconds, claiming the *maillot jaune* by a minute twenty-one.

In a year to forget, Pocagar had delivered a ride to remember.

Bibliography

BOOKS

Andrews, Guy, and Dubash, Rohan *Bike Mechanic* (Rouleur, 2014)

Armstrong, Lance, *It's Not About the Bike* (Yellow Jersey, 2001)

Bacon, Ellis and Birnie, Lionel, *The Cycling Anthology Volume One* (Peloton, 2012)

Bacon, Ellis and Birnie, Lionel, *The Cycling Anthology Volume Two* (Peloton, 2013)

Bacon, Ellis and Birnie, Lionel, *The Cycling Anthology Volume Three* (Peloton, 2013)

Bacon, Ellis and Birnie, Lionel, *The Cycling Anthology Volume Four* (Peloton, 2014)

Bacon, Ellis and Birnie, Lionel, *The Cycling Anthology Volume Five* (Peloton, 2014)

Bacon, Ellis and Birnie, Lionel, *The Cycling Anthology Volume Six* (Peloton, 2015)

Boardman, Chris, *The Biography of the Modern Bike* (Cassell, 2015)

Boardman, Chris, *Triumphs and Turbulence* (Ebury, 2016)

Boulting, Ned *How I Won the Yellow Jumper* (Yellow Jersey, 2012)

Cavendish, Mark, *At Speed* (Ebury, 2013)

Clemitson, Suze, *Ride The Revolution* (Bloomsbury, 2015)

Clemitson, Suze and Fairhurst, Mark, *P is for Peloton* (Bloomsbury, 2015)

Connor, Jeff, *Wide-Eyed and Legless* (Simon and Schuster, 1988)

Cossins, Peter, *Alpe D'Huez* (Aurum, 2015)

Cossins, Peter *The Monuments* (Bloomsbury, 2014)

Elliot, Malcolm, *Sprinter* (Pelham, 1990)

Fallon, Lucy and Bell, Adrian, *Viva La Vuelta! 1935-2013* (Mousehold, 2013)

Foot, John, *Pedlare! Pedlare! A History of Italian Cycling* (Bloomsbury, 2011)

Fotheringham, Alisdair, *Reckless: The Life and Times of Luis Ocaña* (Bloomsbury, 2014)

Fotheringham, Alisdair, *The Eagle of Toledo* (Aurum, 2012)

Fotheringham, William, *Bernard Hinault and the Fall and Rise of French Cycling* (Yellow Jersey, 2015)

Fotheringham, William, *Cyclopedia* (Yellow Jersey, 2010)

Fotheringham, William, *Fallen Angel: The Passion of Fausto Coppi* (Yellow Jersey, 2009)

Fotheringham, William, *The Greatest: The Times and Life of Beryl Burton* (You Caxton, 2019)

Fotheringham, William, *Merckx: Half Man Half Bike* (Yellow Jersey, 2012)

Fotheringham, William, *Put Me Back on My Bike: In Search of Tom Simpson* (Yellow Jersey, 2002)

Fotheringham, William, *Roule Britannia* (Yellow Jersey, 2005)

Fournel, Paul, *Vélo* (Rouleur, 2012)

Friebe, Daniel, *Mountain High* (Quercus, 2011)

Froome, Chris, *The Climb* (Viking, 2014)

García Sánchez, Javier, *Indurain: A Tempered Passion* (Mousehold, 2002)

Hamilton, Tyler and Coyle, Daniel, *The Secret Race* (Bantam, 2012)

Howard, Paul, *Sex, Lies and Handlebar Tape* (Mainstream, 2008)

Kelly, Sean, *Hunger* (Peloton, 2013)

Kimmage, Paul, *Rough Ride* (Stanley Paul, 1990)

Krabbé, Tim, *The Rider* (Bloomsbury, 2002)

Leonard, Max, *Lanterne Rouge* (Yellow Jersey, 2014)

Maso, Benjo, *The Sweat of the Gods* (Mousehold, 2005)

Millar, David, *Racing Through The Dark* (Orion, 2011)

Millar, David, *The Rider*, (Yellow Jersey, 2014)

Moore, Gerry, *The Little Black Bottle* (Cycle, 2012)

Moore, Richard, *Étape*, (HarperSport, 2014)

Moore, Richard, *In Search of Robert Millar* (HarperSport, 2007)

Moore, Richard, *Slaying the Badger* (Yellow Jersey, 2011)

Moore, Tim, *French Revolutions* (Yellow Jersey, 2001)

Nicholson, Geoffrey, *The Great Bike Race* (New Edition)(Velodrome, 2016)

Pearson, Harry, *The Beast, the Emporer and the Milkman* (Bloomsbury, 2019)

Rendell, Matt, *Kings of the Mountains* (Aurum, 2002)

Rendell, Matt, *The Death of Marco Pantani* (Weidenfeld and Nicolson, 2006)

Riis, Bjarne, Riis: *Stages of Light and Dark* (Vision, 2012)

Roche, Stephen, *Born to Ride* (Yellow Jersey, 2012)

Sykes, Herbie, *Maglia Rosa* (Rouleur, 2011)

Thomas, Geraint, *The World of Cycling According to G*, (Quercus, 2015)

Velominati, *The Rules* (Sceptre, 2013)

Voet, Willy, *Breaking the Chain* (Yellow Jersey, 2001)

Walsh, David, *Inside Team Sky* (Simon and Schuster, 2013)

Walsh, David, *Seven Deadly Sins* (Simon and Schuster, 2012)

Wegelius, Charly, *Domestique* (Ebury, 2013)

Wheatcroft, Geoffrey, *Le Tour: A History of the Tour de France* (Simon and Schuster, 2003)

Whittle, Jeremy, *Bad Blood* (Yellow Jersey, 2008)

Wiggins, Bradley, *My Time* (Yellow Jersey, 2012)

Woodland, Les, *The Yellow Jersey Companion to the Tour de France* (Yellow Jersey, 2003)

Yates, Sean, *It's All About the Bike*, (Bantam 2013)

MAGAZINES

In my research, I also referred to back issues of various cycling magazines, in particular *Cycling Weekly*, *ProCycling* and *Rouleur*.

WEBSITES

Lots of great cycling sites on the web. I found the following particularly useful:

Bicycling.com
Bikecult.com
Bikeforums.net
Bikeraceinfo.com
Cyclingnews.com
Cycling-passion.com
Cyclingrevealed.com
Cyclingtips.com
Cyclingweekly.co.uk
Inrng.com
Itsallaboutcycling.com
Pezcyclingnews.com
Podiumcafe.com
Rouleur.cc
Velominati.com
Velonews.competitor.com
Wheelsuckers.co.uk

Acknowledgements

Cycling is a team sport and so is writing a book. I'm very grateful to everyone who has helped play their part in getting *BESPOKE* to publication.

This book has had a long road to publication, with almost as many twists and turns as the climb up Alpe D'Huez. The original version was written back in 2016, but the team I was cycling for at the time, Velodrome Publishing, lost its sponsor and was withdrawn from the starting line within weeks of publication. After various false starts, I was delighted when it was picked up by the British Library and given a new print date of June 2020, to tie in with that year's Tour de France. I think we all know how 2020 went. Updated again, it will now, apocalyptic events notwithstanding, finally see light of day this year. Fingers crossed.

Huge thanks to John Lee, the *directeur sportif*, whose idea this book was in the first place. I've known John for many years and it is lovely to finally be able to call myself one of his authors. Thanks, too, to Neil Stevens, an illustrator with both elan and panache, and as nimble on the overall design front as Pantani was up the slopes.

Many thanks, too, for work on the layouts by Elaine Hewson and Georgina Hewitt. I'm also very grateful to Anna Cheifetz, the road captain of a copy editor, whose subtle editorial hand has improved this script enormously. And likewise to Guy Pearson for his editorial spots. I am very grateful to Charlotte Wilson at Offside for researching the inspiring black and white photographs which appear in this book. Also at the British Library, I'd particularly like to thank Maria Vassilopoulos and Thomas Irvine for their fine efforts on sales and publicity.

Thanks, as ever, to my long-suffering family for, putting up with me as I've been beavering away working away on this book: Joanna, Josephine and Eleanor. And finally to my Dad, for suggesting we sit down and watch the Tour de France back in 1987.

To you all, *chapeau!*

Index of Entries